civil
partnership
A Guide to the Perfect Day

Gino Meriano and Mike Meriano

NEW
HOLLAND

Published in 2009 by New Holland Publishers (UK) Ltd
London • Cape Town • Sydney • Auckland
www.newhollandpublishers.com
Garfield House, 86–88 Edgware Road, London W2 2EA,
United Kingdom

80 McKenzie Street, Cape Town 8001, South Africa
Unit 1, 66 Gibbes Street, Chatswood, NSW 2067, Australia
218 Lake Road, Northcote, Auckland, New Zealand

10 9 8 7 6 5 4 3 2 1

Text copyright © 2009 Gino Meriano and Mike Meriano
Copyright © 2009 New Holland Publishers (UK) Ltd
Gino Meriano and Mike Meriano have asserted their moral
right to be identified as the authors of this work.

A catalogue record for this book is available from the
British Library.

ISBN 978 1 84773 323 8

Publishing Director: Rosemary Wilkinson
Publisher: Aruna Vasudevan
Editor: Julia Shone
Copy-editor: Luisa Moncada
Editorial Assistant: Cosima Hibbert
Design and cover design: David Etherington
Production: Melanie Dowland
Reproduction by Pica Digital Pte. Ltd., Singapore
Printed and bound in India by Replika Press

The paper used to produce this book is sourced from
sustainable forests.

CONTENTS

ACKNOWLEDGEMENTS

We would like to thank the following people for their help and support for this book:

Our best team Oya, Ben and Matt.

Best man and woman, Peter and Alison Greatorex.

Trevor Love – without you we would never have had the perfect ceremony, thank you being our friend.

Brummie birds, Susan and Sharon, for your support and kindness.

Heather and Mark, we wouldn't be able to do half the things we do without your friendship.

Our sister Sandra and little Tina, our most loved niece.

James (JimBob) and Karen, who we love for their kindness and support over the pond in Arizona.

Kyros Michael, just the best.

Lisa, our lush bling lady, who we love passionately.

Zoe, Nicky and our boy Will, who we love and cherish for ever.

Tom – Ryder Boy, the coolest dude around – thank you for always being there.

Andy Webb, not just a friend but the man behind the lens.

Dixie and Fonda, our favourite drag queens, who have never let us down.

The regulars in Cafe One who always keep us grounded – you know who you are.

Our cat Java for reminding us who's really in control.

Thank you Aruna, our publisher, for finding and guiding us into print and Julia for putting up with us and making sure our 't's and 'i's were kept straight.

All our couples.

The venues and suppliers who have supported us over the years.

Trustees and management of the National Trust.

FOREWORD

I have always held the firm belief that same-sex relationships should be legally recognised and fully accepted in society.

In 2001, the year in which I proposed to Mike, I decided to find out what options were available to us to start planning our wedding – assuming, that was, Mike said 'yes'. Luckily, he did and our research began in earnest. After a few glasses of wine, several takeaways and a few very late nights it became brutally clear to us that there was nothing in the marketplace to help gay couples, like us, make such commitments.

After searching many wedding sites and looking through relevant books, it was evident that this was an area that had been seriously ignored and that something had to be done to enable same-sex couples to show their love and commitment to each other in a way that was not just meaningful, but legally binding as well. In 2002, Mike and I launched Pink Weddings™ Ltd, a social enterprise offering wedding services exclusively to the gay and lesbian community.

Why did we call it Pink Weddings™? Well, it certainly wasn't for all the 'fluffy' bits usually associated with weddings, or the stereotypical representations of gay people. We chose the name because of the hidden meanings behind the words 'pink' and 'weddings', the things that most people usually don't consider when they use the term. They are as follows:

Pink
The choice of this word reflects the struggle for gay rights and refers to the way in which gay people have

been subjected to discrimination throughout history. One of the most telling examples of this was in Nazi Germany during the mid-1930s. People considered sub-human (mostly Jews), politically suspect or sexually deviant were either killed or sent to concentration camps. Prisoners were forced to wear a label on their jackets, the colour of which categorised them according to their 'kind' or crime. While Jews wore a yellow star and political dissidents wore red, men, accused of being homosexual, were forced to wear a pink triangle (*Rosa Winkel* in German).

Our use of the word 'pink' in our company name shows our respect for all those who have fought and even died for us to enjoy the rights that we have in society today and pays tribute to the solidarity of the gay community.

Weddings
- A social event at which a ceremony of commitment is performed.
- A party of people at a wedding.

Thus, the combination of the words 'Pink' and 'Weddings' seemed appropriate to Mike and me, and so our company was born.

Over the past few years we have seen some dramatic changes in society, shifts in attitude and legislation that neither Mike nor I would have imagined possible within our lifetimes. In 2004, we witnessed the introduction of a proposed new law called the Civil Partnership Bill, one that would give same-sex couples like us the right to make a more formal and legal commitment to each other.

Mike and I campaigned fiercely for the introduction of the Civil Partnership Act and after receiving Royal Assent, Civil Partnerships finally became legal on 5 December 2005.

One of the most unexpected moments in our lives occurred in early 2005, when we received a call from our dear friend Trevor Love, from Brighton and Hove register office in Sussex, asking if, on 21 December 2005, Mike and I would like to be one of the first couples in the England to hold a Civil Partnership. In one fell swoop, our own wedding was set to go down in history!

On the day itself, Mike and I duly excitedly signed the register at 8 a.m. on the dot. This was followed by a ceremony to show our love and commitment to each other in front of 40 of our closest friends ... and, as it happened, a good deal of the world's press, as well. It wasn't quite the small affair we had hoped for, but it was – as Mike now proudly refers to it – our 'Nelson Mandela Moment'.

In writing this book, Mike and I want to help anyone considering a Civil Partnership to understand what it means in both reality and under the law. We also aim to give you sound advice on how to create a truly perfect day that you and your partner will really enjoy.

—Gino Meriano

HOW TO USE THIS BOOK

On 5 December 2005, the Civil Partnership Act came into force in the UK. It allowed gay and lesbian couples the right to give notice, hold a Civil Partnership and finally have their relationship legally recognised. The Civil Partnership Act gives gay and lesbian couples pretty much the same rights as opposite-sex couples. The key differences are that you can't call your union a 'marriage', there are places where you can't hold your Civil Partnership and it's still not legally recognised in certain countries around the globe (*see Overseas gay weddings, pages 49–51*), but apart from that, to all extents and purposes, it's the same, and it is a huge step forward in terms of gay rights.

In 2005, over the course of three days (19 December in Northern Ireland, 20 December in Scotland and 21 December in England) the UK allowed same sex couples to register their Civil Partnerships. In fact, between 5 and 31 December 2005 we saw a fantastic number of couples, 1,901 to be precise, form a Civil Partnership: the first year alone saw 18,059 registered in the UK (Office of National Statistics (ONS), July 2007), which only demonstrates the true passion and commitment behind a Civil Partnership and the meaning that it has to the couples themselves, their families and friends.

What is even more amazing is that we have seen 27,000 Civil Partnership ceremonies take place in the UK (to the end of 2007), securing around 54,000 people with legal acknowledgement of their committed relationship.

In the following sections we will take a closer look at the various stages necessary to form a Civil Partnership. The Essential Information section (*see pages 13–30*), will help you sort out the nitty-gritty, the formal requirements necessary to forming a Civil Partnership and outlined above. It will also flag important related issues of which you should be aware when undertaking this commitment. The Planning, Choosing suppliers and Making the day happen sections (*see pages 31–116*) will give you a checklist of what to do in terms of arranging your perfect day. The listings found from pages 120 to 126 include our recommended venues, suppliers and other key information.

In addition we have supplied 'WEB*links*' in the margin, which provide details of useful sites, reports and organisations that may further help you. We have also supplied 'TOP *tip*' margin boxes, based on our experience as wedding consultants and as people who have undergone a Civil Partnership ourselves. Finally, there are also dedicated boxes focusing on particular features and details.

Forming a Civil Partnership is easier than many people think but there are certain key processes which you must undertake. In writing this book we have not only endeavoured to simplify matters to get you to the day itself but also to share our own experiences and help you enjoy your day as much as we did on our own.

Publisher's Note: To the publisher's knowledge any statistics cited in the text were correct at the time of publication.

Chapter 1
ESSENTIAL INFORMATION

*'Grow old along
with me; the best is
yet to be.'*

– ROBERT BROWNING, WRITER

To view the Civil Partnership Act in its entirety, go to:
http://www.opsi.gov.uk/acts/acts2004/ukpga_20040033_en_1

WEB *link*

WHY DO IT AT ALL?

Prior to 2005, when the Civil Partnership Act came into being, commitment ceremonies and religious blessings (*see The signing and the ceremony, pages 42–45*) gave same-sex couples the opportunity to demonstrate their love and commitment in the presence of their family and friends. Although these beautiful days were extremely popular, they still came at a price – no legal rights.

This has changed since the Civil Partnership Act came into force, however, and people are now accorded specific legal rights when they have a Civil Partnership signing and ceremony. But many people still ask – why bother doing it?

The following section looks at that question.

Love
Many people claim that there should be one reason and one reason alone for having a Civil Partnership ceremony, that is, LOVE, and that is true. Love is, of course, the main reason that people choose to have a Civil Partnership.

But we don't just include couples in the first flush of love in this category, as these ceremonies allow those people who have been together for years in a long-term relationship and never had a chance to commit legally to each other before the Civil Partnership Act was passed, to have their union recognised in this way.

In the eyes of the law
The passing of this law has improved gay rights and also changed legal history in allowing so many couples to enjoy having their partnership finally recognised by

the law. This means, among other things, that our partnerships are recognised in the event of the death of a partner and that we can inherit property and money, for example, as legally recognised spouses. This is, for many people, one step closer to gay relationships being fully accepted by mainstream society as just another form of commitment between two loving people, irrespective of sexuality.

We will look closely at the full legal implications of entering into a Civil Partnership later in this chapter, giving valuable information on such issues as prenup agreements (*see page 21*), inheritance tax (*see page 23*), wills and estates (*see pages 24–27*), responsibility for children (*see pages 27–29*) and changing your names (*see pages 29–30*).

This chapter of essential information also gives you all of the crucial details you and your partner will need to arrange your Civil Partnership signing and ceremony. You will find advice on contacting your local register office, giving your 'notice of intention' (*see pages 17–18*) and eligibility requirements to hold a Civil Partnership (*see pages 18–20*). You will also find information on the logistics of arranging a Civil Partnership if you or your partner live outside of the UK (*see Who can do it?, pages 19–20*), as well as many TOP *tip* and WEB*link* margin boxes, designed to make this whole process easier to organise.

Correct some misconceptions

It is a misconception that gay people do not have long-term or serious relationships: in fact, this is far from the truth. The Civil Partnership Act finally enables us to legally recognise this and allows same-sex couples to show just how committed they are to each other.

WEB *link.*
To view the Wolfenden Report, see the office of Public Sector Information
http://www.opsi.gov.uk/RevisedStatutes/Acts/ukpga/1967/cukpga_19670060_en_1

Before this it was very different: even after the 1957 Wolfenden Report (*see* WEB*link*), which led to the decriminalisation of homosexuality in Britain in 1967, gay couples living in stable relations had done so without any legal, financial or societal recognition.

However, now Civil Partnerships are one of the most beautiful ways of showing your love and commitment to your partner in front of your family and friends.

... And also be part of our history
Mike and I passionately believe that every same-sex couple that places names on the Civil Partnership register is another name that goes down in history.

This shows that we have finally broken down another stereotype about our community, allowing people to see that we are equal and have the same feelings and desires to commit to each other as any opposite-sex couple.

HOW TO GO ABOUT ARRANGING A CIVIL PARTNERSHIP

Although the Act has been in force for several years now, many couples still find it difficult to work their way through the procedures. Common questions are: *What do we need to do? Who do we need to speak to? How much will it all cost?* The essential question is, however: *Is it very complicated to arrange a Civil Partnership ceremony?*

The answer is a resounding 'NO!' ... and here's why:

* The first thing to do is set a date. Remember your Civil Partnership signing can take place at any time of the year, except Christmas Day, Boxing Day and New Year's Day, between the hours of 8 a.m. and 6 p.m
* Then contact your local register office (*see* WEB*link*) to check the availability of that date and make an appointment to give your 'notice of intention'.
* When you give notice you must produce identification, usually a current passport or a birth certificate, along with supporting documents like a driver's licence, Council Tax document or medical card. In addition, you must show proof of residency and also show that both of you have lived in the UK in a registration authority for at least 7 days prior to giving notice of your intention to register your Partnership. Each person must give notice individually (*see box, page 20*).
* Once you have given notice, you have a waiting period of 15 days (14 in Scotland) before you are

WEB *link*

For a list of designated register offices go to:
http://www.gro.gov.uk/gro/content/civilpartnerships/index.asp

TOP *tip*

If your Civil Partnership is to be registered outside of your area of residence, you and your partner will still need to give notice in the respective borough or boroughs in which you live.

able to hold your Civil Partnership signing and ceremony. From the time you give notice the application is valid for a one-year period.

❋ When you give notice of your intention to register a Civil Partnership, details from the notice will be available in a register office for public inspection (as in the case of a marriage) but the details will not include either the address or addresses of you or your partner, unlike in the case of an opposite-sex marriage.

❋ It is important that these details are publicly available during the 15-day waiting period in order to allow for any objections to be made, just as in the case of marriage. The grounds for objection to a Civil Partnership are the same grounds for objection to marriage: for example, someone could object if they think the couple are not eligible to register a Civil Partnership (*see box below*).

This is pretty much all you need do in terms of paperwork. Now that's out the way, the fun and games can begin and you can start planning your perfect day by following the pointers we give in this book.

Civil Partnership eligibility requirements

What do you have to do to be eligible? You must both:

  ❋ Be of the same sex.
  ❋ Not already be in a Civil Partnership or marriage.
  ❋ Be 16 years of age or older.
  ❋ Not be within the prohibited degrees of relationship.

In England and Wales individuals aged 16 and 17 have to obtain the written consent of their parent(s) or legal guardian(s).

WHO CAN DO IT?

As soon as you start thinking about planning your Civil Partnership, it's always good to know if there are any legal restrictions on who qualifies to have one. There are a number of formalities that always come with any Civil Partnership and these must be investigated and completed before you can begin to enter into one. The information in this section may help you to work out if you and your partner qualify.

In the UK
People living in the UK can form a Civil Partnership as long as they fall within any of the following categories:

- They are of the same sex.
- Neither is already married or in a Civil Partnership with someone else.
- They are over the age of 16 (if they are under 18 they will require parental consent).
- They are not closely related to one another.

Outside of the UK
People residing outside of the UK must be able to fulfil the following requirements to hold a Civil Partnership in the UK borders:

- They must have Entry Clearance expressly for the purpose of enabling them to form a Partnership in the UK – a Partnership or Fiancé(e) Visa in their passport. This must be obtained from a British Embassy or High Commission in the country of origin; or,
- They must have been granted indefinite leave to remain in the UK and this must have been stamped in the relevant passport; or,

✻   They must have a Certificate of Approval, which
     must be applied for by post from the Home
     Office. It costs £135 for each Foreign National
     and is valid for 3 months. Any enquiries about
     applying for the Certificate of Approval must be
     made to the Home Office on + 44 8706 067766.

Once this is done you are ready to give your notice
of intention to form a Civil Partnership and you and
your partner must attend a designated register office
to 'give notice' (*see box below*). At this stage you will
need to bring all required documentation with you,
including proof of identity, otherwise the notice
cannot be taken.

Notice of intention made simple: Q & A

Q: *I live in Weybridge and my partner lives in Kent, but I really want
to register my Civil Partnership at the fabulous Eastlands Estate in
West Sussex. What do I have to do?*

A: Give notice to your local register office in Weybridge and
your partner also has to do the same thing at the Kent register
office, near to where he or she lives. Now you have given notice,
you can both book the date and the place where the Civil
Partnership is to be registered, i.e. West Sussex, in this case.

LEGAL IMPLICATIONS

When becoming Civil Partners, you and your partner will have the same rights as married couples. The only exception to this rule is adultery, which is a specific legal term relating to heterosexual sex and which cannot, therefore, be used as grounds for dissolving a Civil Partnership. If your partner is unfaithful the grounds for dissolution would be cited as unreasonable behaviour instead.

When choosing to have a Civil Partnership, there are several factors you need to consider carefully. If you want both of your wishes taken into account with regard to such matters as your financial and health decisions, property and children, for example, you need to ensure the correct documentation is drawn up. This section looks at some of the key issues:

Prenup agreements

These might be fashionable and may serve to focus the mind of the participants, but as yet they carry surprisingly little legal weight in the UK. At present, any such agreement entered into by a couple is a factor the Court may consider when making a financial order upon the Civil Partnership ending but it is not legally binding and cannot override the Court's discretion to make different financial arrangements on dissolution. However, there are various steps the parties can take to ensure their prenup agreement is given as much weight as possible:

1. The couple planning to register a Civil Partnership should:

    ※ Each seek their own independent legal advice before entering into an agreement.

✲ Each fully disclose to the other a true picture of their financial means and circumstances, with a summary of such means being attached to the agreement.

✲ Bear in mind that, on dissolution, a Court looking to review an arrangement will want to see if it leads to a fair division, on a basis of equality and if not, why not?

2. The agreement should:

✲ Make clear how any assets each partner is taking into the Civil Partnership are to be held in future and how they will hold any new assets acquired.

✲ Address how the equity in the home will be divided and who will occupy it if the relationship breaks down.

✲ Address how their assets are to be divided up in the event of the death of one of them.

✲ Be entered into not less than 21 days before the Partnership signing.

Your finances

Among the factors you need to consider seriously are your financial circumstances, especially if there is a great deal of disparity between the amounts you each earn or the assets you own separately. There are so many questions that need to asked and answered by one or both of you and touching on this subject can be tricky.

Some of the issues you need to address are:

✲ Who you wish to protect in the event of your death?

✲ Who will ultimately inherit?

* What will happen in the event of death, illness or new relationships after your current one has ended, for whatever reason?

With the above in mind, consider the following issues:

* Inheritance tax.
* Funding of long-term care.
* What protection you can offer your partner financially if he or she forms a new relationship after your death.

TOP *tip*

We highly recommend www.direct.gov.uk to find out more about Inheritance Tax and Civil Partnerships. It gives you information in easy-to-understand language, without the legal jargon.

Be sure to find reliable companies (e.g. PinkWills.com; *see page 27*) who will have your best intentions at heart and will make sure your needs are catered for. You need to appoint someone who will manage your affairs in the event of your possible mental incapacity, for example, and who will be able to make health treatment decisions for you if you are unable to.

Prior to the Civil Partnership Act, many same-sex couples were treated in the same way as opposite-sex couples that were unmarried, but this has changed. When you come to register your Partnership, as far as your Will is concerned, you will be given the same rights as married couples (*see Wills and estates, page 24*).

Inheritance tax (IHT)

One of the most commonly asked questions by gay couples contemplating a Civil Partnership is: *Should I pay IHT?* Others are: *What is IHT?* and *Why should it concern us?*

Well, not everyone pays IHT on death. It only applies, if the taxable value of your estate (including your share of any jointly owned assets and assets held in some types of trusts) is above £312,000 (2008–2009 tax year). It is only payable on the excess above this nil-rate band. This is a generic term for the point at which the tax threshold for IHT is reached, ie: amounts ranging between £0.00 and £311,999.99. Each person within the Partnership is allowed to inherit up to £312,000 without any liability for IHT; the rate is therefore set at 0 percent, hence it is called the 'nil-rate band'.

There are also a number of exemptions that allow you to pass on amounts (during your lifetime or in your Will) without any IHT being due. For example: if you are both residents in the UK and the estate held by you and your partner passes to you in the event of your partner's death, there will be no IHT payable, even if the value is over £312,000. However, there will be action to be taken on the second death relating to possible liability so legal advice should be sought. Most gifts made more than seven years before your death are also exempt. Certain other gifts, such as wedding gifts and gifts in anticipation of a Civil Partnership up to £5,000 (depending on the relationship between the giver and the recipient), gifts to charity, and £3,000 given away each year (unspecified gifts to anyone) are also exempt.

It is good to have an idea of your transfers into trusts and companies as they are subject to an IHT charge if they exceed the nil-rate band (taking into account the previous seven years' chargeable gifts and transfers).

Wills and estates

Once you have held a Civil Partnership ceremony, any existing Wills need to be updated. A Civil Partnership renders null and void any previously written Will and/or estate plan, and if you fail to update any existing Wills you would effectively die intestate (with no Will). One option is to prepare a document 'in anticipation of a

Civil Partnership', providing the intended date of your
Civil Partnership signing can be supplied and adhered to.

You should be aware that in the event of dissolution of
a Civil Partnership, your former partner will be omitted
from the Will and/or estate plan and no gift will pass
onto them after your death. They also cannot act as
executor, if named in your Will. The residue of any such
Will and/or estate plan will remain valid, however.

A common misconception

Many same-sex couples believe that when you register
your Partnership you gain equivalent rights to those that
are held by married heterosexual couples, inasmuch as
you automatically inherit your partner's estate upon
death if there is no Will stating evidence to the contrary.
A common misconception held by couples in both
groups is that it means you inherit the whole estate. For
Civil Partners and married couples alike the surviving
partner only inherits the first £125,000 and the interest
on half of the remainder, if they are not the only relative.

Children are the automatic beneficiaries of any amount
over £125,000, and if there are no children, but other
surviving relatives, then the spouse receives the first
£200,000 and the relatives equal shares of the balance.
Should the estate be of a size to attract IHT on the
children's inherited amount you should be aware the
IHT bill has to be paid by the children and has been
known to force the sale of the family home to enable
the bequest to be fulfilled.

Scottish law differs slightly as the surviving spouse,
where there are children, will receive the home or a
share of the home up to £300,000 and contents to the
value of £24,000. They also receive cash up to the value

of £42,000. The residue is apportioned amongst the spouse and children but these arrangements are particular to Scotland and remain under review as do those for the rest of the UK due to the impact on the security of the surviving spouse.

Living wills

An adult with full mental capacity can refuse treatment for any reason, even if that might lead to death: they cannot insist any particular treatment is given. This is known as an 'advance directive' and is the only type of 'Living Will', which is legally binding (*see* WEB*link for more information*). Any such 'advance directive' must be extremely specific and precise in its intention, and preferably in writing (*see bullet points below*).

It allows you to refuse medical treatment if you do not want it. If you become so seriously ill that you are unable to communicate and unlikely to recover, or, for example you develop a severe condition, your doctor will normally decide what treatment they think is best for you. However, a Living Will leaves you in control and advises your medical team how you wish to be treated if this situation should arise.

Such an instruction, which intends to refuse life-sustaining treatment, **MUST** be in writing, and there are legal requirements in this circumstance. They are set out by the Mental Capacity Act as follows:

* ✳ It must be in writing, but you can instruct someone else to do that for you if you are unable to do so.
* ✳ It must be signed by you or someone on your behalf in your presence.
* ✳ That signature must be witnessed.

WEB *link.*
See document on advance directives issued by Age Concern October 2007:
http://www.ageconcern.org.uk/AgeConcern/Documents/ISSAdvancedecisionsOct2007.pdf

※ You must include a written statement that you intend it to apply to a specific treatment even if that puts your life at risk.

It is illegal to ask for the following:

※ Euthanasia or assistance to commit suicide.
※ Treatment considered inappropriate by your healthcare team in your circumstances.
※ To refuse the offer of food or drink.
※ To refuse basic care such as provision of warmth, pain relief or shelter.
※ To refuse basic nursing care eg: washing, bathing or oral care.

It is advised that if any alteration is made, all copies of a previous Living Will are destroyed to avoid confusion.

Our friend Sue Elkington, from PinkWills.com, has been helping Pink Weddings™ and our couples for over six years, and has always been on hand to offer advice and practical bespoke plans from simple Wills to Trust creation and management of high-value Estates including Property and Offshore Planning for effective Portfolio Management.

Responsibility for children

Not everyone who lives with or looks after a child has an automatic legal responsibility for him or her. Having legal responsibility for a child is called 'parental responsibility'. It means that you can have a say in the child's healthcare, education and welfare and over whether the child can be taken abroad.

A woman who has given birth to a child has automatic parental responsibility. So does a man who was married

WEB *link.*

For a valuable source of additional information on legal responsibility for children, visit: http://www.adviceguide.org.uk/index/family_parent/family/civil_partnerships_and_living_together___legal_differences.htm#responsibility_for_children

to the mother at the time of the birth, although he can obtain parental responsibility through other means.

If you're the lesbian or gay partner of someone who has a child or children, you have no automatic parental responsibility for those dependents because it is unlikely that you and your partner will both be the birth parents of the child. Though in a rare circumstance you may find that parental responsibility may exist if one partner has undergone gender reassignment, having been in a standard heterosexual relationship with their new lesbian or gay partner.

If you are in a Civil Partnership, you will become the step-parent of your partner's child. This will not give you automatic parental responsibility for the child, however. You can apply to a court for it though. You can do this whether you and your partner are Civil Partners or just living together. If you are living with your partner, you will not become the step-parent of your partner's child, but you can get parental responsibility by adopting your partner's child (*see* WEB*link for more information on this topic*).

Circumstances equitable to a married/cohabiting couple

If you marry or become a Civil Partner you become the step-parent; you do not become the step-parent if you are just co-habiting, but in either circumstance you can apply to adopt your partner's child.

Under certain circumstances, you can ask a court to grant you a 'contact order' (which allows the child/children to stay with you for short periods of time, at weekends or as part of school holidays) or a 'residence order' (which decides where and with whom the child is going to live) when your relationship (whether it be a Civil Partnership or cohabitation) comes to an end.

The difference between sexes
If you are a woman in a Civil Partnership and your partner has a child, you automatically become a step-parent and can apply for a parental responsibility order. This is not the case if you are a man, however.

Financial support of children
Both birth parents are responsible for supporting a child financially. This applies whether or not they are living together and whether or not a parent has legal parental responsibility. You will also have financial responsibility for any child you adopt. This applies whether you are in a Civil Partnership or just co-habiting with your partner. If you are a step-parent, you will also have financial responsibility for your child. However, you can't be asked to pay financial support by the Child Support Agency (CSA).

Again, we would strongly recommend you make contact with the CSA to explain your situation and see how best they can help you and your partner.

Changing names
With your day fast approaching, you may wish to consider whether you want to change your surname.

What are your options and how do you go about doing this?
The process is very simple and four options available are:

1. You may wish to take your partner's surname.
2. You can merge your names into a double-barrelled surname; for example, Mark Jones

and Paul Sinclair can become Mark and Paul Sinclair-Jones or Jones-Sinclair.
3.   You can completely change your surname via deed poll (*see below*).
4.   You can keep your own original surnames.

Notification

Once you have decided to take your partner's surname or to change it to a double-barrelled name, for example, be sure to notify the registrar before your Civil Partnership takes place (*see pages 17–20*). Like an opposite-sex couple you simply present your Civil Partnership certificate to any legal or financial institution, such as your mortgage company or bank and credit card companies. You must also remember to change it on documentation such as your passport, driving license and the electoral roll.

Deed Poll

A deed poll is a legal document. The correct legal term for this is 'Deed of Change of Name'. This document proves that you have taken a new name and legally binds you to that name. While this document is essentially an English legal document it will be recognised by all government departments, companies and organisations throughout the UK. Once a name change has occurred, you must notify all the relevant authorities. Include a copy of your Civil Partnership certificate and to prove that you and/or your partner have changed names, provide the necessary evidence of the name by which you (both) wish to be known.

An example of this might be: Mark Jones and Paul Sinclair have a Civil Partnership and both change their surname by deed poll to McCallan. They are known thereafter as Mark and Paul McCallan.

Chapter 2

PLANNING

*'Before anything else,
preparation is the
key to success.'*

– ALEXANDER GRAHAM BELL, INVENTOR

INTRODUCTION

It is worth noting that you will be planning your Civil Partnership for quite a few months before the event takes place, if not longer. Mike and I want to reassure you that planning can actually be fun. So, don't let the thought of it send you and your partner into a state of terror, and don't lose interest through boredom.

In our experience everyone involved brings something special to the table. For example, Mike has a particular aptitude for planning: he loves almost everything you can buy at stationery shops, such as binders and those machines that make labels for folders. On the other hand, I prefer more creative jobs. By bringing our complementary skills to the table, as wedding consultants, we have helped our clients turn their dream day into reality, creating truly memorable and fantastic occasions.

The following section will give you and your partner a few key points to think about, such as how long things take to plan (*see pages 33–36*), what type of ceremony to have (*see pages 42–45*) and how to choose your best team (*see pages 52–55*). The advice we give you will help you plan and create your perfect Civil Partnership ceremony and celebration.

In chapter 4, on pages 109 to 114, we supply you with a checklist and a supplier log to make sure nothing gets forgotten. Both of these lists are downloadable from our website using the link and the password given on page 113.

TIME FRAMES: HOW LONG DOES IT TAKE?

So, you have proposed to your partner and he or she has said 'yes'. Now, it's time to set a date and begin planning your Civil Partnership – but how long will it take to make your dream day happen?

An often-asked question from our clients is about the time frame and if it is the same for opposite-sex and same-sex couples. Typically opposite-sex couples allow 10 to 18 months from deciding to get hitched to when they actually have their marriage ceremony – so, for instance, if the proposal took place in October 2008, the wedding would fall on a chosen date between August 2009 to April 2010. But how do same-sex couples compare in the same situation?

A Civil Partnership time frame

Looking back over the Civil Partnerships that Mike and I have helped couples plan in 2005, 2006 and 2007, the typical timescale has been more like 6 to 10 months. At the risk of generalising, same-sex couples have been so keen to secure their long-awaited legal rights that we've moved mountains to arrange the legal signing and a small ceremony quickly. And if you're simply looking to hold the signing and ceremony to secure your rights as a couple, it can be done legally in a matter of weeks (*see pages 17–18*).

In 2007 and 2008, however, we saw increasing numbers of couples wanting more elaborate wedding celebrations. These affairs naturally took longer to pull together and the time taken from proposal to Civil Partnership has crept up towards that of an opposite-sex marriage.

Lead-time
The lead-time to your Civil Partnership ceremony all depends on what you have in mind for your day and what needs booking in advance, including the most important part, the venue. One thing to bear in mind is that most opposite-sex couples are booking venues anything from one to two years in advance. This can cause heartache if you don't plan ahead when you're looking for a specific venue for your day.

The venue
The venue is often the one thing most couples have set their heart on, so a tip is to look at the register office's website for suggestions of where to hold your Civil Partnership and see which venues are licensed before ringing around to check availability and costs.

Ask the venue if they take provisional bookings and how long they will hold the date for you. This will allow you time to view the venue, be sure it's the one for you and also that it fits within your budget.

In chapter 3, we talk more about choosing suppliers (*see page 75*). For now, remember there are many suppliers in the wedding market so allow yourself time to contact as many as possible to gauge prices, availability and whether they need to be booked well in advance of your day.

Checklists
All this planning may seem quite daunting. Don't panic! The best way to start is by creating a simple checklist (*see page 113 to download our version*) of everything you need or would like for your wedding. The list may seem never-ending but trust us when we say it will pay dividends both for your sanity and the success of your day.

Allocating time

Experience has shown us that it pays to allocate time throughout the week and at weekends specifically for planning your day. Keep an eye on how much time you are spending and remember to balance the other things in life that are important to you both.

Friends and family

Something else that can help is to involve your family or friends, where possible. This is a great way to make them feel involved in your special day from the beginning and also gives you crucial help and support, thereby taking a little pressure off what can be one for the most stressful times of your lives (*see Choosing your team, pages 52–55*).

Rewards

Keeping your enthusiasm and energy up is very important so don't forget to reward yourselves when big things are booked, such as the venue. Enjoy some 'you-time' together, such as a dinner at your favourite restaurant – or perhaps even the venue you've booked!

In our experience

Taking our experience into consideration, Mike and I would recommend you allow between 6 to 12 months to plan your Civil Partnership ceremony and remember, once you have the date booked, send out a simple 'save the date' card so that your guests can put it in their diaries and make any necessary arrangements to join you on your special day (*see pages 39–41*).

A wedding planner

If the idea of organising all the elements for your day is too daunting or you are concerned about balancing your career, life and family, then why not engage a

TOP *tip*

Look at the Pink Weddings™ site for more information on suppliers and venues. We have an up-to-date list of people, companies and locations that we recommend. Our team is very happy to give you advice on this subject.

professional wedding planner to take away a lot of the stress and detail planning. This will leave you free to command and direct how you would like your day to unfold. Wedding planners have a great deal invested in making sure the day you and your partner want happens. It is worth contacting a few wedding planners to gauge their ideas and prices. (*see Directory of resources, pages 120–123*). Most official and more expensive venues also have a designated adviser who will work with you to book their recommended suppliers.

Wedding insurance

For peace of mind it is always best to make sure you have wedding insurance to give you some compensation should anything happen to ruin your day. For example, what do you do in the following scenarios:

- ❊   If the photographs don't come out?
- ❊   If one of you falls ill, or worse?
- ❊   The venue closes down?
- ❊   You lose the rings?

What's amazing is you can get this for as little as £49 depending on what you insure against on your day (*see www.weddingsurance.com for further information*).

CHOOSING THE DATE

Dates that are significant or special are probably one of the most popular reasons why people choose a particular day for their Civil Partnership. For example, our date 21 December was the day on which Civil Partnerships became legal.

How important is the date to you and your partner?

There are so many reasons that make a specific date attractive to you. Possible reasons might include:

- ❊ The anniversary of the day you first both met.
- ❊ The date on which you proposed or were proposed to.
- ❊ A special or significant date for you or your partner.
- ❊ A family tradition.
- ❊ An historic date.

Other factors to consider when choosing your date include:

- ❊ The implications of having a wedding in a particular season: Spring, Summer, Autumn and Winter (*see Weather on page 38*).
- ❊ Pick a date because it suits both of you. After all, the date you choose will have its own significance after your Civil Partnership.

No one ever said you have to follow tradition and hold your ceremony on a Saturday. You may find it interesting to know that the most popular days of the week for Civil Partnerships are Thursday through to Sunday.

Weather

The British are renowned for obsessing about the weather, but most people prefer to hold their Civil Partnership in a certain season and the weather conditions are something over which you have absolutely no control. With this in mind you might want to consider at an early stage of planning the following:

- ❋ Fresh spring morning weddings often have backdrops of new blossoms.
- ❋ Summer may bring barbecues, picnics, jazz bands and a glass of Pimms or two.
- ❋ Autumn colours of leaves turning red and orange may appeal to the more daring of you.
- ❋ Winter is a wonderland of magic and excitement draped with ice queens and fake fur.

Each season does bring some disadvantages though. Spring is littered with bank holidays and notoriously unpredictable weather. The long summer days mean fireworks really only work at the very end of your day. Planning outdoor photographs in autumn may mean you have less time or need to find somewhere inside, and while the winter months may have a magical feel this is one of the busiest times for hotels and venues with large groups of revellers booked for festive parties.

Remember planning and booking early may mean you don't have to balance or compromise on your chosen place or date. But whichever date you choose, it will be a wonderful experience for you and your partner.

SAVE THE DATE CARDS AND INVITATIONS

The concept of inviting guests to a wedding has evolved over the years. Picture the days when a Town Crier walked the streets shouting announcements to the community of an impending wedding and those in earshot became part of the celebration. Today, things are quite different and it's up to you to send invitations typically through the post or, increasingly, via email to your chosen guests.

Back in 2005, there was an endless choice of printed invitations for opposite-sex couples but until Mike and I began working with a few supportive cardmakers, none were aimed at Civil Partnerships. Now you will see some in the high street and more online through specialist wedding stationery suppliers (*see pages 120–123*). With so many options now available it's all about creating the look and feel that matches the theme for your day.

Do take care when ordering invitations online: many couples have found out the hard way, ordering invitations online by simply seeing the design and choosing the colours, only to find out it doesn't match their theme and end up being disappointed. When looking for a supplier, choose carefully:

* Be sure to see samples and get quotes.
* If a company is not happy to send samples then contact another.

Save the date cards

These cards have become very popular and are used to notify the guests that your special day is coming and to 'save the date'. They give people plenty of notice, allowing them to make any necessary arrangements while they wait for the proper invitation giving all the details of your day. This also removes some of the pressure of setting a time frame for sending out invitations when everyone on your list is aware of the day well in advance.

Invitations

When you have chosen the design for your invitation how should you word it?

Trying to work out how to word your invitation can be tricky but whatever you decide to choose, make it as personal as you want: there is no established etiquette and, as same-sex couples, there are no years of tradition to draw from. What we do have is our own style and, in turn, we can create our own tradition. The world is your oyster, so be as adventurous as you want.

Mike and I had the following invitation, which had some traditional elements:

It's our day.
Gino and Mike
Would like to invite you to our wedding
21st December 2005
for our
Civil Partnership and Ceremony
7.30 a.m. on the dot
Brighton Register Office

Champagne breakfast
9 a.m. till 3 p.m.
Chartwell Suite
Hilton Metropole
Brighton
RSVP

As the vast majority of Civil Partnerships are planned by couples themselves, traditional wording often goes out of the window. However, you can always adapt a traditional invitation, such as the example below, to suit a Civil Partnership:

Mr and Mrs D. Jones
request the pleasure of your company
to celebrate the marriage of their daughter

Rachel Elizabeth
to
Andrew Brown

to be held at St James Church, Weybridge,
on Saturday 10th April, 2010, at 2 p.m.

The reception afterwards will be held at
The Oatlands Park Hotel, Weybridge, Surrey

This invitation can be easily adapted for a Civil Partnership. For example:

Jason and Steve
request the pleasure of your company
to celebrate their Civil Partnership

to be held at the Cheshire Register Office
on Saturday 10th April, 2010, at 2 p.m.

Something a little bit different

Many same-sex couples want something a little different, fresh or even humorous. This may include touching and personal, fun or romantic words, sometimes with a spiritual slant. Previously used examples include:

* ❄ 'Please join us for a celebration of love, friendship and laughter'.
* ❄ 'To celebrate our partnership together'.
* ❄ 'Join us as we pledge our life commitment to each other'.
* ❄ 'For the blessing of our unity'.

THE SIGNING AND CEREMONY

Legal acknowledgement of same-sex relationships is still new in many European countries and not even considered in many other countries around the world (*see Overseas gay weddings, pages 49–51, for information on countries that so far recognise Civil Partnerships*).

While full recognition in society may still be something we all can work towards as a future goal, who would have thought four years on that we would already have so many choices for ceremonies?

At first sight, you may think the only option for you and your partner is to have a Civil Partnership signing and ceremony conducted by the register office. In fact, you are only required to have a registrar conduct the signing. This means you can choose to add a fantastic ceremony, ranging from secular or religious to spiritual. In the sections that follow we outline some of your options.

Choosing the ceremony

TOP *tip*

If you choose to have a separate ceremony, we recommend you have the legal signing first.

Signing the register without a ceremony
This is where you would simply sign the Civil Partnership register in the presence of a registrar and two witnesses held at the register office. It's as simple and quick as that.

A register office ceremony
No religious elements may be incorporated into the ceremony. A Civil Partnership ceremony conducted by a registrar may include readings, music of your choice (nothing overtly religious: just because 'God' may be mentioned does not automatically preclude its inclusion – for example the National Anthem is allowed) and the

exchange of vows. It is also worth noting that ceremonies may vary, depending upon the Registration District. These ceremonies can only be conducted at the register office or in a licensed venue.

A different approach

Why not take a different approach to arranging your ceremony? The following will give you a taste of what is available to help make your ceremony that much more personal and meaningful for you and your partner.

An independent celebrant ceremony

A commitment ceremony is a meaningful and dignified affair. Each commitment ceremony is unique and offers you a huge range of options, including using your own personal words, poems, readings and music tailor-made for you and your partner.

Unlike the register office ceremony, this can be held anywhere and does not have any restrictions on either the venue or the content. Spiritual and religious aspects may also be incorporated, depending on your celebrant.

A religious ceremony

Currently, there are a few widely recognised religions that have specific ceremonies for same-sex couples, for some, it is left to the discretion of individual priests or ministers to conduct.

Since the introduction of the Civil Partnership Act many religions have struggled with accepting same-sex couples and their rights. For example, the Church of England was divided in its response to the legislation. Unlike opposite-sex couples, a legal church wedding is still not permitted or recognised for same-sex couples. Liberal Judaism was one of the first faiths to come on board and open its arms to same-sex couples. While it is unable to offer a legal blessing it has been widely accepted by the community alongside many other alternative-faith-based organisations. We hope the following list helps you when it comes to deciding on a ceremony that suits you and your partner.

Interfaith ministers

Interfaith ministers embrace the universal truths found in all authentic spiritual paths, regardless of distinctions such as age, health, race, gender, nationality, religion or sexuality. Perhaps a more fitting title for them would be 'People's Ministers' as they aim to serve the evolving spiritual needs of today's colourful and vibrant gay and lesbian society. The wonderful thing about People's Ministers is that they serve people of all faiths, no faith whatsoever and any variation of belief in between!

The opportunity of holding a spiritual ceremony, blessing or commitment ceremony removes any obligation to use particular language or symbology that doesn't fit for you. Nor are you restricted as to what you would like to have included. Be as creative or traditional as you like and see your own ceremony come together, using only those elements you personally find fitting and meaningful.

Religious blessings

One of the key differences between same-sex and opposite-sex ceremonies is that we do not have the option of a legal church wedding. Despite this there are many wonderful choices available to augment the signing of a Civil Partnership. Organisations like the Metropolitan Community Churches (MCC) can offer you all the elements of a traditional blessing, including the lighting of candles, singing of hymns and Bible readings. Scattered around the United Kingdom you will find a selection of MCC venues in which you may have your blessing (*see Directory of resources, pages 120–123*).

If you're looking for a venue be sure to ask if they will allow a priest or minister to be present to perform a religious blessing.

Jewish 'weddings'
Rabbis from Britain's significant Jewish community were one of the first mainstream religious groups to authorise gay marriage services. Liberal Judaism has produced liturgy and a Covenant of Love that can be held before or after your Civil Partnership signing.

The ceremony follows the same format as a traditional Jewish wedding service under the 'chuppah' (or canopy) along with the ceremonial breaking of glass symbolising sadness at the destruction of the Temple of Jerusalem and identifying the couple with the spiritual destiny of the Jewish people.

The Rabbi will explain and recommend any changes to the ceremony, such as:

※ A same-sex version of the seven blessings said at heterosexual Jewish weddings: the seven blessings may be read or chanted, or seven friends and relatives may be invited to offer their own blessings to the couple. For more information please see the Liberal Judaism book, *Covenant of Love* (London, 2005) or the WEB*link* in the margin.

※ Exchanging the words '*Sheva Berachot*', meaning 'Bride and Groom' with '*re'im ahuvim*', meaning 'loving couples'.

WEB*link*

For more information on the seven blessings go to:
http://www.ou.org/wedding/7brachot.htm

CHOOSING A VENUE

Your venue is the heart and soul of your Civil Partnership: it will encapsulate what your day is about and help create memories for you; it will echo with the sounds of laughter of your family and friends and be the backdrop of everything you remember for years to come.

Making sure you have found the right venue may seem like a very hard job (*see* TOP *tip*).

While the first place to look is the register office website, as we have already mentioned (*see The venue, page 34*), also ask friends and loved ones for suggestions; especially those who have recently got married or held their Civil Partnership. Look at magazines and scour websites (*see Directory of resources, pages 120–123*). This is an important decision that is central to making your day perfect and so it is vital that you make an informed choice.

TOP *tip*

For a list of recommended venues, please look at the Pink Weddings™ website. All of our venues are tried and tested and we will only list places that we feel are beautiful and provide a great service.

Key questions to ask yourself

※ Does the venue have the feel and look you want for your day?

※ Does it need much to decorate it in the style you want?

※ Will it accommodate the number of guests you have in mind?

※ And, most importantly, does it fit within your budget?

Once you have these questions in mind, it's time to make contact with the selected venues and take a tour of each to see firsthand what that particular venue has

to offer and find out what the actual prices will be as
you start to plan your ideal day.

When you meet with the hotel events or wedding
organiser be sure to have a list of questions you would
like to ask. It's important to get as much from him or
her at the first meeting to help you decide if it is the
right venue for you. Remember that even though venues
arrange many weddings and Civil Partnerships every
year, this is your day and so you should be made to
feel special and that they care.

It's important to build a rapport with the venue and the
people you meet there. They will both help you create
your perfect day and also be at your Civil Partnership to
ensure everything runs smoothly without you or your
partner having to worry.

Key questions to ask the venue or wedding organiser

A simple guide to help you start your planning and
to enable you to ask those important key questions
might be as follows:

* Is there a room charge?
* Is there a payment plan and what deposit is
  required to secure your date?
* Are there any additional or hidden costs within
  the contract?
* When choosing an historical building, what
  limitations and restrictions are there, if any?
* If you do not want to use the venue's caterers
  and suppliers, will there be additional costs?
* What's included in the meal price per head?
* What about any requests for children and guests
  with special dietary requirements?

❊   How late does the license run for? Will there
       need to be an extension if you want the evening
       to run later?

❊   Where are the best places to have pictures taken?

❊   Is there a dance floor and how quickly can the
       room be turned around from day to night?
       This should normally only take about half an
       hour to do.

❊   Will there be a manager present on the day to
       oversee the wedding and ensure all runs
       smoothly? If yes, be sure to get their contact
       details and ask that they make themselves known
       to you and your partner before the day.

❊   Is there a room in which you can change?

❊   Is there accommodation available either in the
       venue or close by for any guests wishing to stay
       the night? If not, can the venue recommend tried
       and tested places?

❊   Is there parking and is there a charge?

❊   Can you have fireworks? Always check if the
       venue will allow fireworks as some may not due
       to sound restrictions? Did you know you can get
       soundless fireworks now?

❊   If you choose to bring in your own champagne,
       will there be a corkage charge at the venue?

TOP *tip*

*Do not sign
anything until you
have read it
through in detail.
Ask questions if
there are things you
do not understand.*

If all of your requirements are met, book a date. The
venue will then send out any necessary paperwork for
you to sign and will usually ask for a deposit, which
may or may not be refundable (*see* TOP *tip*).

OVERSEAS GAY WEDDINGS

The idea of flying to an exotic country and planning your special day under the guarantee of the sun, soft white sand under your feet and the amazing backdrops the world has to offer is not only exciting and enticing but a reality for most opposite-sex couples. You may be surprised to find that combining an overseas gay marriage ceremony and celebration with your honeymoon destination could cost a fraction of an equivalent Civil Partnership and celebration here in the UK (*see* WEB*link*).

However, when it comes to same-sex unions, our options are limited and our relationships are not universally legally or morally recognised around the world. While the UK has joined many other countries in offering same-sex couples the opportunity to legally bind their relationship, some countries only allow residents to do so, or dictate that at least one member of the couple must be a resident. What does this mean for you? It limits the number of countries to which you can travel in order to hold a legally binding ceremony.

We also have a long way to go before every country accepts same-sex couples. Mike and I joke about our travels and the point at which we should remove our wedding rings when entering a country that does not recognise us as a couple. As the rest of the world slowly catches up with countries like the UK, there are still some amazing places for you to consider – with beautiful scenery and warm welcomes to make your day wonderful. Since going to print, Canada, South Africa and Gran Canaria have all opened their doors to same-sex marriages and to anyone wishing to have his or her ceremony in these countries.

WEB *link*

Go to the Foreign and Commonwealth Office website to find out what is needed when planning your wedding overseas: *http://www.fco.gov.uk/en/travelling-and-living-overseas/ta-relevant-to-you/overseas-weddings*

Nations recognising gay marriage:

Canada*, Belgium, Netherlands, Norway, South Africa*, Spain, Gran Canaria*

US states recognising gay marriage:
Connecticut, New Jersey, New York, New Hampshire, Massachusetts

Nations recognising same-sex partnerships or unions:

Croatia, Denmark, Finland, France, Germany, Hungary, Iceland, Luxembourg, Mexico, New Zealand, Norway, Portugal, Sweden, Switzerland, United Kingdom*

US states recognising same-sex partnerships or unions:
New Hampshire, Oregon, Vermont, Washington

* countries that will allow anyone around the world the right to hold a legally binding marriage or Union within their borders.
** on 5 November 2008 California lost this right.

On a serious note, there are countries, 77 to be precise (November 2008), where it is still illegal to be homosexual. Even enlightened countries, such as North America, where homosexuality is not necessarily illegal, can, on occasion, present a very confusing picture depending on which state you're in. For example, although New York recognises and accepts couples that have entered into a gay marriage or Partnership, it does not actually offer such ceremonies in its own state.

Some countries have given same-sex couples the right to marry, thereby changing the definition of the word 'marriage' ('the formal union of a man and woman, typically recognised by law, by which they become husband and wife'; *Concise Oxford English Dictionary*, 2008), while other countries offer a Partnership or Union that gives couples the same rights as marriage but stays clear of using the word. It is important to find out the legal stance in the country of your choice.

A beautiful island, but a problem for same-sex couples

While the lovely island of Jamaica may cater for many newlyweds it is also known as one of the most homophobic destinations in the world. Would we recommend it for your Civil Partnership ceremony or honeymoon? That depends on how much you want to visit the island. It is better to know the facts about any destination before you book and there are other more gay-friendly locations that you might consider.

Popular honeymoon destinations

Just the mention of a honeymoon is more than likely to conjure up something magical for you. You may have a favourite destination in mind like a beach in Thailand or the city life in San Francisco. Perhaps it is an adventure you have always promised yourselves like a safari in South Africa or a bungee jump in New Zealand!

Pardon the cliché, but the world is your oyster – literally. Without wishing to cast a cloud over any plans, we always recommend that our clients check with both the Foreign Office (http://www.fco.gov.uk/en/travelling-and-living-overseas) and Pink Weddings™ for any country/region advice or security warnings. Sadly, in the past, the travel industry has recommended that same-sex couples visit countries where they have subsequently had to 'hide' their sexuality, without letting them know the local sensitivities beforehand(*see box above*).

Wherever you choose for your escape, have fun and make the most of the time you have together to enjoy sights and experiences that you will remember for the rest of your life, whether it be soaring over the Tanzanian Serengeti Plains at dawn in a hot-air balloon or swimming with dolphins in Perth, Australia.

CHOOSING YOUR TEAM

In order to complete the official part of a Civil Partnership – the signing (*see pages 42–45*) – you only need two witnesses, but for your ceremony or celebration, you may want to create a dream 'best team' (the people who are going to help you achieve your dream day). Choosing your best team can be so much fun and this is where you start to plan who does what for your day. So, let the party begin!

Using loved ones – or not?
It is always good to have the people you love involved as little or as much as you like – depending on how well you get on with them and how much stress they may cause you. When deciding who will do what, think about the roles your family and your friends may take and who might be best suited to help make your ceremony special.

Having other people help during the planning of your Civil Partnership and on the day itself may take some stress away from you both. For instance, you need two witnesses to sign the Civil Partnership register with you but you can have different people to walk with you down the aisle. You may also choose to have 'best people' as ring keepers, bridesmaids, pageboys and even dog handlers, for example.

TOP *tip*

Don't be surprised at how diverse your team, helpers and supporters can become. Start with a checklist of roles and jot down who you both would like to help.

Key people
Witnesses
Two witnesses are required by law to sign the Civil Partnership register with you and your partner in the presence of the registrar.

While there are no set rules as to who you should pick to be your witnesses, choose carefully as their names will be on your Civil Partnership certificate. You might like to consider having a close relation like a mother, father, brother or sister or your closest friends.

Best people
Traditionally, the role of the best man is pivotal in making the wedding day a success. There are arrangements to be made, rituals to be observed, courtesies to be extended, and the groom's hand to be held! While some of these responsibilities may still stand, a lot will change for your Civil Partnership. The best man could be a man or a woman or the role could be done by one person or two, thereby making them 'best people'.

For many couples, Mike and I have been 'virtual' best people through getting to know the couple and taking on the duties of the best man. We have ensured the couple's day runs smoothly, people know where they are going, the right people are thanked at the right time, and so on. In fact, this has ended up working out really well for the couple and their guests as they have all been left to enjoy the day fully without anyone feeling the pressure of being the 'best person'.

Equally, however, many friends or loved ones would be honoured to be asked to fulfil this role and having someone that you've known all of your life, or for a significant period, as your best person, may really add to your special day.

Helpers and supporters
Don't be surprised to hear people say: 'let us help'. Friends and family members may be quick to offer a helping hand and while this is a lovely option, be sure to keep a tight rein on what they do, making sure

they actually do it. With the best will in the world, everybody will have their own ideas and themes for your day – none more so than your close family, but it's you and your partner that should ultimately make the final decisions.

Someone you know may well offer to take the 'official' pictures, which could save you money. While we have seen some great shots in our time, we've also seen couples end up with none at all, so before you rule out an independent, professional photographer sit down and honestly discuss how much you want all your guests to enjoy the day. The stress of being the photographer might mean someone really important to you does not enjoy him or herself at your Civil Partnership celebration (*see pages 84–88 on photographers*).

Remember also when you decide to engage a close friend or family member as a supplier, you have to approach the way in which they provide that service in the same way you would if they were an independent supplier and this may cause potential problems.

Use as many people close to you as you need, even to run errands or help with final touches leading up to your day, as this is a time when friends and families should come together and help you and your partner ensure that every detail has been seen to and nothing has been overlooked.

When knee deep in planning, a fresh pair of eyes won't hurt, just in case you have missed something off your checklist (*see pages 110–113*). Remember, if it looks like your day is spiralling out of control, don't rule out a wedding planner's or a hotel co-ordinator's advice and help (*see Directory of resources, pages 120–123*).

TOP *tip*

Give away disposable cameras to children on the day. Make them official 'snappers'. This not only makes them feel more interested in the proceedings, but can also produce some fantastic shots.

The happy couple:
Nicky and Zoe's best team

Nicky and Zoe have chosen their initial team:

- ❋ Their fathers have been chosen to walk their respective daughter down two aisles (*see pages 57–59*).
- ❋ Both mothers will be the witnesses and sign the Civil Partnership register.
- ❋ Nicky and Zoe have decided that they also want bridesmaids and page boys and split the six chosen to follow them down the aisles, three to follow Nicky and three to follow Zoe.
- ❋ Darren and Claire, the best friends, are the chosen 'best people'.
- ❋ Mark, a close friend of the family, will be the 'ring keeper'.
- ❋ Heather will give the guests the order of the ceremony.

So, at the beginning of our involvement in Nicky and Zoe's celebration, they already have 14 friends and family members involved in the ceremony alone.

When we started to plan their day an added twist came into the mix: the couple's dog, Skye, became the 'best bitch'. She wore a designer collar to match the day's theme!

All in all, that's 14 people, plus Skye the dog, and, oh, let's not forget the two most important people, Nicky and Zoe, so that's 17 people, involved in the Civil Partnership signing and ceremony alone.

Moving onto the celebration, however, more people joined in. Zoe's grandmother was brought in to make the centre pieces for the tables and the flower decorations. Nicky's uncle baked and decorated a stunning cake and a friend from college, who happened to be in a band, performed a number of songs as part of the evening's entertainment! All of these people made the day much more special for Nicky and Zoe.

TRADITION VS TREND? ... YOU DECIDE

Tradition has always played an important part in the overall concept of opposite-sex weddings, but for same-sex couples it is perfectly appropriate to think outside the box. Fresh, innovative ideas will inspire your guests, create new experiences for both you and your partner and even change the way in which you regard accepted traditions, thus forging new paths for weddings of the future.

Since the introduction of the Civil Partnership Act, many of the couples we have helped ask questions about trends and traditions. These include:

* Is there some sort of formal etiquette?
* Who walks down the aisle first?
* Is there a need for a top table?
* Should I have a drag queen or toastmaster?
* Who makes a speech?
* Is there a line-up?
* Do I have to have photographs in a album?
* How can I make my cake unique?

Actually, there are no hard-and-fast rules and the really exciting concept behind organising a Civil Partnership is the wonderful fact that there are no traditions or formal etiquette that couples need to follow: the overall wedding format and look can be whatever the couple desires. The following section looks at the ways in which you can make your day different – from having two aisles and whether to have a drag queen rather than a toastmaster to original ideas about seating plans and top tables.

ONE AISLE ... OR TWO?

Around six years ago when we first started to plan commitment ceremonies, blessings and celebrations we didn't imagine that concepts would change very much in the world of wedding planning. As the years have gone by, however, we have realised that there is so much more to learn than we had initially anticipated and, as a result, there is so much scope for new and innovative ideas.

Five years ago we were asked to help two ladies arrange a commitment ceremony in Lancashire, England, and after meeting with them and their families it became apparent that both ladies wanted to experience the age-old tradition of having their fathers walk them down the aisle. One of the fathers talked to me about his feelings on weddings when he found out his daughter was gay. He explained that, although perhaps selfish, one of his first thoughts was that he would not get the chance to walk his daughter down the aisle and have the wedding he wanted for her. Mike and I wanted to make sure that we brought his dream, as well as his daughter's, to reality.

How could we get two women and their fathers to walk down a single aisle and make it work?

Helping to fulfil dreams

First of all, we cleared a room and laid out chairs and placed a table at one end so that we could plan how to help these ladies and their fathers achieve their dream. We discussed which father would walk which lady down the aisle and where the bridesmaids, page boys and flower girls would go. Once all of that was decided, we had to deal with the issue of the single

TOP *tip*

Why not add an aisle runner to your ceremony or celebration. Personalised for you and your partner, colour themed to match your day or simple and stylish for that final touch to your walk way or entrance (see pages 120–123).

WEB *link.*

For ideas on aisle runners visit:
http://www.aislerunner.eu

aisle, but then it came to us: why stick with tradition and just have one aisle? Why not have two?

By placing the chairs for friends and family in the middle of the room, there could be room for two aisles running down each side. But once that was done, another question arose: how could we make sure that both members of the family got equal billing and had their proper share of the limelight?

We agreed that one father and daughter would walk to one side of the room first and when they were halfway down their aisle, the second father and daughter would then begin making their way down their aisle (*see illustration opposite*). In this way, both the ladies and their fathers got the limelight they desired and enjoyed their moment of walking down an aisle. Each father also had the great pleasure of passing the hand of his own daughter over to her partner.

But we decided that, to spice it up a little, one of the ladies would have just girls follow her down the aisle and the other would have just boys.

It was, without doubt, one of the most touching moments that we have experienced in creating a commitment ceremony and we were immensely proud to have been part of this couple's day and to see the ceremony unfold with our new concept working so beautifully in practice.

This idea can be adapted and you can have any member of your family or any friend walk you down the aisle.

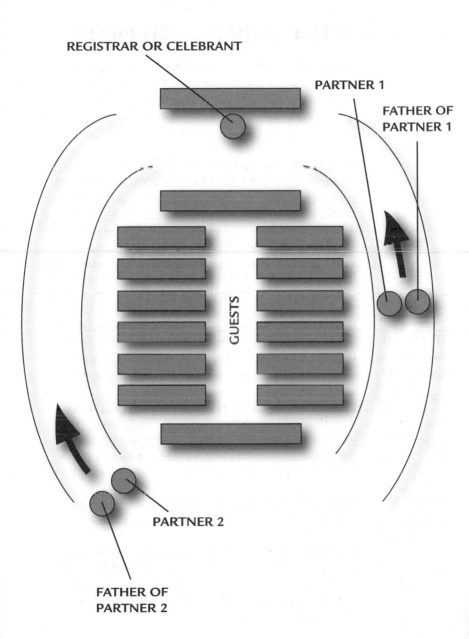

A TOP TABLE ... OR NOT?

A top table has been a traditional part of opposite-sex celebrations for many years now. However, today, more couples are looking at ways of modernising the well-established 'long table', or are simply looking to adjust the seating plan to suit the happy couple.

Traditionally, the top table is invariably a straight (no pun intended) table at which the wedding party sits, placed to face the guests. This gives guests the opportunity to see the wedding party, listen to the speeches and also allows the couple to see all their guests. Alternatively, on occasion, people have simply adopted the David and Victoria Beckham approach, which is to have a table all to themselves. This creates a sense of grandeur, especially when using high-backed, throne-style chairs.

TOP *tip*

Try changing the centrepiece to make your table look different to your guests' tables, thereby making it clear that it's a special 'couples-only' table. For example, if your theme is silver and blue, alternate the colour scheme making your table blue and silver from the flower arrangements to the favours. It will look great and it really does work.

In practice, we haven't had to create a traditional top table for that many of the Civil Partnerships that we have helped organise. The most popular choice is to have a series of round tables at the wedding reception.

When you have picked your table, which usually seats 8 or 10 people, it really is up to you and your partner who sits with you. Unlike traditional opposite-sex weddings, etiquette has no real place here and you have more choice and flexibility.

Where should the top table go?

You can have so much fun with this. For example:

The centre of the room: If you don't mind that half your guests will be looking at your back. What works well for a wedding party of around 50 is to keep 2 spaces free per table, allowing the happy couple to move between tables throughout the meal. However, this can be time consuming and tiring.

A round table: The best and most frequently used option is to choose a round table situated in one of the corners of the room. This will give you the best view of everything and everyone. This gives you a top table but it's not obvious that you have one.

The traditional top table: There is nothing to say that you can't go down the traditional route, but don't make it complicated. While the format may remain the same you may end up substituting the best man and chief bridesmaid's seats for the 'best people' (*see page 53*), or the line up could include the best person, chief bridesmaid and the two witnesses (if they don't include your parents).

Whatever you decide, make sure you're sitting with the people you both want to be near. It's your day!

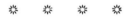

Mike and I have found that using a different centrepiece to differentiate your table (*see* TOP *tip opposite*) is an informal, personal and intimate arrangement. It removes the formalities usually associated with having a long, rectangular top table and creates a feeling of togetherness. Even though there is, in fact, some form of a top table, this idea allows both the couple and their guests to feel part of the wedding reception, while still maintaining the couple's special position.

When you have decided where your table is going to be situated, you will need to spend some time planning the seating arrangements for your guests (*see* TOP *tip*).

TOP *tip*

Make arranging the table plan fun by creating a sketch of who sits where and play with it till both you and your partner are happy.

TOASTMASTER ... OR DRAG QUEEN?

Since the introduction of Civil Partnerships we have seen many changes and twists to the actual day and none more so than the toastmaster versus drag queen debate. Now, we know what you're thinking but before you say 'no, surely not!' and dismiss it out of hand, allow us to explain why you may want to consider having a drag queen rather than a toastmaster.

A trendy vs more traditional approach: what's best for you?

They may well be worlds apart in their approach and style but both the toastmaster and the drag queen have a shared common aim – to make sure your day runs smoothly. When required, they can make the announcements and help your guests be in the right place at the right time. The real difference is only in look and approach as the master of ceremony.

A respected drag queen in the gay and lesbian community tends to be professional, courteous and has a particular charm that brings excitement to the room. A drag queen will help with all the main duties of the day and has that extra something that can add an unusual twist to your Civil Partnership day.

How? you may ask.

Well, why do your day guests have to wait for the evening reception before they have some form of entertainment? Let your drag queen add that extra wow-factor at the end of the reception and spill into the evening segment.

Let her, for example, introduce a range of comic turns, live vocals, sing-alongs or even get her to be the DJ for the night. The drag queen's talents are varied and whatever she does it's always stylishly performed.

A traditional master of ceremonies

On the other hand, the red-coated toastmaster, as the master of ceremony, discreetly goes about his or her duties and provides you with the reassurance that all is in hand for your day.

The toastmaster lends an air of British tradition to the proceedings that adds a more formal touch to your Civil Partnership. His or her duties remain the same as those outlined, but also may act as an adviser, organiser, diplomat or even your event liaison.

Lady toastmasters are proving very popular for Civil Partnerships. Often with years of experience, a good female toastmaster mixes the old with the new but adds a different dimension, that touch of being a woman. It still surprises guests that you can have a lady toastmaster, but let's face it – anything stylish and unique is a great talking point at your Civil Partnership.

Fonda Cox, a dear friend of ours, makes the perfect Queen of Ceremonies. As the day's events come to a close, Fonda takes over and entertains the guests with a comedy song hour, which includes some classic songs such as Judy Garland's 'Over the Rainbow', Abba's 'Dancing Queen' and Kylie's 'Can't Get You Out of My Head', to name but a few.

When it's time to start the disco, Fonda is also a great DJ and will easily fill the dance floor for you until the early hours of the morning.

Lady toastmaster Lynne O'Hara and toastmaster Michael O'Hara, have been working with couples for over 10 years now. They offer ongoing help and support leading up to the day including advice on:

- ❈ A running order.
- ❈ How you should meet your guests.
- ❈ When and where you should cut the cake.
- ❈ How the speeches will take place.
- ❈ The form of any introductions and announcements.

Lynne and Michael have always been on hand to help opposite- and same-sex couples, and are more than willing to adapt their services to make sure you get the very best from them.

One thing to bear in mind is always find out as much as you can about the toastmaster you are planning to use. To ensure you are booking someone noted for their work, it helps if he or she is a member of an association such as the National Association of Toastmasters (see WEB*link*).

So, it's tradition or trend and, in the words of a popular reality show, '*You decide*'!

Remember to look at pages 120–123 for lists of useful resources that will help you at this planning stage.

WEB *link*.
To find out more about toastmasters visit:
http://www.natuk.com

SPEECHES

How many good or bad speeches have you heard at weddings?

No matter what your own feelings are towards a speech or two, some say that this is the part where you get to share your own important experiences and your lives with those you love and also, perhaps more importantly, hear from the people that matter to you and your partner.

It's still a fact today that preconceptions and stereotypes surrounding gay relationships persist. Mike and I have, on a number of occasions, seen these creep into a couple's day in the form of overtly gay, 'pink and fluffy' or inappropriate references about sexuality. There is a very fine line between being humorous and offensive and this is something that you and your partner should discuss with your chosen speechmakers in advance, making it clear what's acceptable to you and what's not.

For many gay couples, the term 'family' actually refers to more than just blood relatives. When talking about 'family members', we mean parents, brothers, sisters and close friends. One thing to remember is that while we know we have families, others may forget and it might be helpful to gently remind speechmakers that your grandparents or younger family members may be present and to think about this fact when writing speeches. Things they may find funny, your family may not.

Some traditions still have a place and speeches can be one of them – the only question really, is who should deliver them?

TOP *tip*

Remember your Civil Partnership is as important both legally and emotionally as a marriage, however don't feel you have to include gay history in your speech.

Order of speeches

In opposite-sex marriages, the father of the bride usually goes first, followed by the groom, after which the best man makes his speech. So, let's look at this in more detail and see how it can be adapted for the purposes of a Civil Partnership. Then, it's up to you to decide on what you want and who you want to speak.

Parents of the bride

Traditionally the father of the bride speaks. His speech focusses on the life of the bride up until the moment she marries. It is usually quite sentimental and involves anecdotes, jokes and tributes to the bride.

Over the years we have seen many variations of this in same-sex ceremonies: the first and probably the most obvious is when a close member of the respective families speaks about each of the partner's lives – for example, it could be a brother talking about his sister and a mother talking about her daughter.

TOP *tip*

An unexpected way to open your speech is to parody the 'groom's traditional opening' statement 'on behalf of my wife and I'. Change this to suit you and your partner. For example, two men might use 'on behalf of my husband and I'. You will be amazed at the reaction it causes, especially the laughter.

A popular variation is, as in the case of our first double aisle couple, when both sets of fathers want to do a speech on behalf of their daughters or sons, or mothers on behalf of their children. You can have great fun with this and talk through with your parents about the best way to deliver this. For example, both speakers could perform a double act, which not only could be entertaining but also might be a fun surprise for guests expecting traditional marriage speeches. This may even bring both families closer together or break the ice.

The groom's speech

Traditionally, this speech is the chance for the groom to thank the bride's father, his new mother-in-law, the guests and family; to give presents and thank the bridesmaids, best man and ushers; and also to pay tribute to his new wife. This is essentially where, for same-sex couples, the fun begins, as one or both of you can stand up and make the speech (*see* TOP *tip opposite*). If you decide that one of you will speak on behalf of you both then choose the person that feels most comfortable doing so.

Don't forget to thank everyone that is present, those who could not make it and any loved ones that have passed away. Make special thanks to the people that have helped you through the key stages of planning (*see Choosing your team, pages 52–55*). You don't have to be funny or come out with jokes. You can keep it simple, poignant and express how important the day is for you and your partner. This is a special time especially now you stand in front of the people you love most, finally united in your partnership, recognised by law.

The best man or best people

We have all experienced best man's speeches that are light-hearted and occasionally go over board on stories about the groom's past. If you decide on a best person, or even two (one for each of you; *see page 53*), factor in time to speak to him, her or them about the speeches.

We all know that making public speeches can be very nerve-wracking but if your best person has never been to a Civil Partnership before, they may not have an idea of your expectations, so try to help them as much as possible. The people you choose love you and will want to do everything possible to make your day special and get it right.

Share a glass of wine as you recall possible funny encounters or events that they could recount in their

TOP *tip*

When serving bubbly on your day, try replacing the traditional strawberry in the glass for 2 blueberries. They may be easier to refresh your palate at the end of the glass perhaps also it will be a bit of a talking point when handed to your guests.

Some 'do's and 'don't's for speeches

❋ Good public speakers use the 3 Ps – Prepare, Practice and Perform.

❋ It's good to be nervous but try to have fun doing it.

❋ Don't underestimate your emotions on the day so even if you are a confident 'off-the-cuff' speaker, our advice would be don't try to wing it on this occasion.

❋ When having two best people, get them to share that role equally, from making the speeches to reading any best wishes and cards.

❋ If you have asked anyone to give a speech, careful thought and planning always helps as speeches can be both eagerly anticipated and dreaded at the same time.

❋ Remember to brief your speechmakers on what you want them to say as well as what you don't.

❋ Make it clear what's offensive to you.

speech about you or you and your partner together. Gently remind your speechmaker that they should really only use anecdotes that are suitable for the wide range of ages and backgrounds of your guests.

Giving advice to the chosen ones

Be prepared for some questions from your chosen speechmakers and be honest and upfront about what you think.

Whether your speechmakers suffer from stage fright or are worried about making sure it's done right, the important thing is that what they will say are words from the heart. Remind them that it's not an audience in a theatre they will be speaking to, but some of the closest and dearest people to you and your partner, and they will only commend and support you or them through the speeches.

A carefully planned speech can take as long as three weeks to create. Make sure that you prepare far enough in advance to have time to go back to make changes and additions where you see fit. The person writing it will know when he or she has done everything possible to make the speech fantastic.

It's always tempting to add gay or straight jokes to the speech; the choice is the writer's but aim to balance this with the importance and significance of the couple's commitment to each other.

Consider how long a speech will take. It will help to set time limits: usually 5 to 10 minutes is more than adequate for each speech. You may think that's quite short – it's not, honest! Try it out for yourself and see.

However you decide to arrange your speeches remember to let whoever may be introducing the speeches know. Whether you consider a toastmaster, a drag queen (*see pages 62–64*) or a co-ordinator for your day, don't be stifled by accepted opposite-sex marriage etiquette – unless it is right for you.

COSTS AND BUDGETS

One of the most stressful things about planning a Civil Partnership is the budget. *How do you find out how much something should cost? What do you get for that? What should you receive as standard, and what do you have to pay for as an extra?* This section helps you come to grips with what you should expect to pay for various services (at 2008 prices) and gives you a breakdown of what you can expect for a budget of about £1,000 and one of about £20,000.

The differences between opposite-sex and same-sex budgets

The average cost for an opposite-sex wedding is around £20,000 (Source: *You & Your Wedding* magazine's National Cost of a Wedding Survey, 2008) but when we take a closer look at Civil Partnerships we notice the trend to be somewhat different.

Know how far your money stretches

Your budget is paramount in planning your Civil Partnership and it's important to understand that while you don't have to fit into any particular bracket, it's always good to know what the market is charging when it comes to paying for your day.

We have known couples arrange their day for as little as £1,000 (*see box on page 71*) but Civil Partnership trends are emerging showing two price brackets as more common: £5,000 to £7,000 and £13,000 to £15,000. There are a few, and I mean a very few – around 150 – that fall into the over £45,000 range.

Trends have also shown that an average party for a Civil Partnership consists of either around 40 people or over 80 people.

A Civil Partnership for less than £1,000

Mary and Kat really wanted to have their special day but money was the key issue because they were also starting a new family. They were able to keep costs down and do what they wanted by having the reception in their back garden, borrowing a marquee from a friend, making their own invitations and buying outfits with vouchers kindly given by friends and family for Christmas. The official photographer was a friend and they also asked their guests to bring along their cameras.

In the end, through the kindness and generosity of friends and family, everything was pretty much provided for the day, including the cake. The local community centre lent them tables and chairs for the reception, while Mary and Kat handled the catering themselves.

All in all, the day was amazing, proving that you can plan for your day and keep the costs down.

Venue, drinks and menu

When you start planning your day's events, one of the first things you need to look at is how much the venue, menu and drinks will cost.

Does the venue have special offers or any additions that will help keep your Civil Partnership within budget? It's always good to ask if the venue has any package deals. Sometimes you will find these to be a great option to use that could cover most, if not all, of your needs for the main part of your celebration.

For example, listed following are two completely different styles of venues, number of guests and packages offered by an urban hotel and an upmarket country hotel and

TOP *tip*

Check the register office website for approved venues, select the ones you like and call each of them for quotes and available packages. Once you have this, it will be easy to determine the ones that are within your budget and the ones that have to be removed.

TOP *tip*

Search the internet; it's amazing what you can source for your day at prices that are often far better than those of retail stores.

from this you will be able to see how the number of people covered, style and menu vary between venues.

120 guests for less than £5,000

For example, based on a minimum number of 120 guests, the Holiday Inn, Camden, North London, has been known to offer the following package at a price of £40 per guest:

- ✳ Venue hire.
- ✳ Three-course meal with half a bottle of house wine per guest.
- ✳ A glass of sparkling wine per guest for toasts.
- ✳ A table plan and place cards.
- ✳ A complimentary executive room for you and your partner (including a full English breakfast).

Taking this into account, you have just spent £4,800 without even thinking about extras, such as evening canapes, entertainment, etc. Not a bad start from just one phone call!

50 guests for less than £6,000

Now, what if you decided to go for a privately-owned historic country house – let's say the Oatlands Park Hotel in Weybridge, England, which was once the site of a grand Royal Palace of Tudor King Henry VIII (1491–1547; reigned 1509–1547) and his daughter Queen Elizabeth I (1533–1603; reigned 1558–1603).

You have a wedding party of 50 guests and the venue offers a package price of £114 per person. Therefore you are spending £5,700, including VAT, for the following:

- ✳ An experienced wedding organiser to co-ordinate your arrangements.

❊ Red carpet.

❊ Arrival drinks.

❊ Selection of canapés.

❊ Main room hire for wedding breakfast and evening reception.

❊ Elegant menu cards and matching place cards for you to write.

❊ Wedding breakfast, for example:
  Cured Scottish oak-smoked salmon, red onion and caper salad.
  Free-range chicken breasts, filled with tomato, basil and mozzarella mousse, fondant potato and rosé wine sauce.
  Strawberry vacherin with passionfruit cream.
  Half a bottle of wine and mineral water per person.
  Glass of champagne to toast.
  Coffee and petit fours.

❊ Use of our silver cake stand.

❊ A complimentary cake knife memento for the couple.

❊ Evening buffet.

❊ Professional toastmaster.

❊ Allocation towards flowers – normally around £4 per head which would give you a nice table decoration included in the price.

❊ Complimentary bedroom with four-poster bed for the couple and a champagne breakfast delivered to your room.

❊ Full English breakfast for all Oatlands Park Hotel residents in your party.

❊ Free car parking.

Costs can easily mount up and before you know it you could end up losing control (see TOP *tip* box). At times it may seem like you're comparing apples with oranges

TOP *tip*

Always ask the venue if there is a minimum number of guests required in their package prices as this will have an impact of your budget.

but the best way to tackle this is to jot everything down on your checklist (*see pages 110–113*) and then see what your best options are.

This may sound obvious but its surprising how confusing it can become, when you're wrapped up with planning your special day and ideas are flowing. Make sure you prioritise the things that are most important to your day.

£20,000 in the blink of an eye

Can you imagine being faced with average costs like:

Engagement ring:	£729
Wedding dress:	£661
Photography:	£353
Catering:	£2,285
Drinks:	£551
Cake:	£189
Reception venue:	£1,423
Flowers:	£204
Transport:	£228
Honeymoon:	£2,007
Other:	£3,023

(Source: *You & Your Wedding* magazine's National Cost of a Wedding Survey, 2008)

You will easily have spent £20,000 before you know it, when in fact a careful eye over the arrangements could reduce this price without comprising quality. That's where a good Civil Partnership or wedding consultant will be able to assist you and get the very best rates possible and even on occasions pass discounts directly to you and your partner.

Chapter 3

CHOOSING SUPPLIERS

*'Perhaps the feelings that
we experience when we
are in love represent a
normal state. Being in
love shows a person
who he should be.'*

– ANTON CHEKHOV, WRITER

INTRODUCTION

When the time is right, you need to start finding suppliers that will help create your day and add all the touches you have been planning for. The question is, where do you start? You may have heard some horror stories about couples calling suppliers and being told 'No! We don't cater for "your sort" here'.

Times are changing – but perhaps not quickly enough

It's hard to believe that in this day and age, we still see around 19 percent of suppliers in the wedding industry saying 'no' to Civil Partnerships. In doing this, they are totally disregarding the Equality Act (2007) that is supposed to protect us from this kind of discrimination. Don't be put off as this is a minority, behaving illegally, and they are far outnumbered by suppliers who are more than happy to offer their services and who obviously don't have a problem with a couple's sexuality.

What can we do?

To help you avoid such unpleasantness, Mike and I have built up a collection of Pink Approved™ suppliers over the last six years, that have been checked and verified and who we feel have your best interests at heart. We have helped them with their own questions about the differences between opposite-sex weddings and Civil Partnerships to ensure they can offer the very best service to you and your partner (*see* WEB*link*).

Ask questions to get answers

When looking through websites (*see Directory of resources, pages 120–123*) be sure to give any prospective supplier a call and ask as many questions as you like. Don't feel

WEB*link***.** For more information on our recommended suppliers visit: *http://www.pinkweddings.biz/goodies.htm*

put off or uncomfortable in querying things as it's your day and everything must be to your liking.

Key questions to ask might be:

- ❋ How long have you been in the business?
- ❋ How many Civil Partnerships have you dealt with?
- ❋ Can you supply testimonials or references?
- ❋ Do you have public liability insurance?
- ❋ What can you offer us that other similar companies can't?

The Pink Guide, part of the Guides for Brides group (*see* WEB*link*), set up a website to help couples look for suppliers when planning their Civil Partnership. We loved the way they handled this. They asked us for the facts and created sections to offer help and support and they contacted every supplier on their books and asked them if they wanted to be listed in the Civil Partnership section. Believe it or not a few refused (yes, in this day and age…), but the ones that said 'yes' are listed and are passionate about helping us.

A supplier should be willing to offer his or her services and sexuality should be irrelevant, but remember this is a relatively new market and on occasion the odd slip up will happen. It doesn't necessarily mean that suppliers are homophobic however; it's just for years they may have been dealing with the 'Bride and Groom'.

Attitudes are changing, but sometimes it just doesn't seem fast enough for us, as a community. That's why we hope that the following sections of this book and the advice that we give you will make your path to your Civil Partnership that much easier and enjoyable.

WEB *link*

For help in looking for suppliers visit:
http://www.thepinkguide.co.uk

CATERING

Food and drink are things that take up a lot of time when arranging a wedding. *What should you have? Where should you start? How much should you budget for?*

You will need to find out if any of your guests has special dietary requirements. Remember that 'vegetarian' means just that and not that people eat fish or white meat. Vegans are another case altogether. Other people may have wheat or dairy intolerances. Also remember that children may not be willing to eat what you eat.

Most venues will either have their own chef and catering staff or give you a list of their approved caterers. While at first this may seem like it takes away your choice, our experience is that you can still discuss the menu with the chefs and, depending on your budget, have precisely the food choices you wish.

If your venue permits external caterers ask about the kitchen facilities, cleaning arrangements and food restrictions that may be in place, so that you can let your caterers know.

When it comes to choosing a catering company, let your taste buds direct you! Over the years Mike and I have arranged menus ranging from the cool and contemporary through to hearty and home-style cooking.

Trends

A growing trend in wedding catering is Ethnic Fusion, which combines amazing tastes from across the globe with the passion of chefs preparing the food right in front of you, your partner and your guests. This not only adds spice to your food, it also adds to the entertainment.

Choosing wine and beverages

As a rule of thumb allocate around half a bottle of wine per person at a sit-down meal.

Based on 50 adults at your Civil Partnership you would be looking at 25 bottles of wine. Roughly divide this up between red and white. Some tables may drink more than others but this usually means you will be able to use the wine you have allocated elsewhere, as you want, and reduce the number of new bottles of wine being opened, thus avoiding unnecessary additional charges.

For those that don't drink why not offer a range of non-alcoholic wines that are not only great in taste but also show your guests that you have thought about them, over and above providing just orange juice and water.

Alternatively, many chefs also offer a fresh, frugal approach to the catering scene using an eclectic range of tempting nibbles and canapés with a light, healthy buffet and salad bar.

Whether you decide to tie your catering into a theme or not, making your menu vibrant, fresh and appropriate to the occasion will have your guests talking well into the evening – and beyond.

Always ask for details of experience from any chefs and caterers you approach and ask about sampling before you commit. In fact, most caterers will invite you into their restaurant to sample their range either free of charge or for a modest or refundable cost.

What's on your cake?

Sometimes just the mention of a wedding produces visions of a traditional three-tiered, fruit-filled and flower-topped style cake, but whereas opposite-sex

TOP *tip*

A cook out or barbecue can be ideal for outdoor celebrations. Many catering companies offer exciting, freshly-prepared and cooked menus that go far beyond burgers and bangers!

Cake tops

Spectacular clay cake tops can transform a cake and become a keepsake for you and your partner for years to come. Picture this: simply send in a photograph of you and your partner, describe what you both will be wearing, your hair colour, and so on, right down to the colour of your nail varnish, the tartan for your kilt or even your favourite pet, then see these details translated into your very own, unique cake top.

A great friend, Jilly, helped us launch a range of same-sex cake tops in the UK and is very well known for her creations. Why not visit our website and take a look (see WEB*link*).

tradition dictates the wedding cake is served to guests at the reception, with a portion kept for the bride and groom's first anniversary or the couple's first-born, we don't have the same limitations.

Many cake artists have the ability to design stunning confectionary that can match your day's theme or create that wow-factor. You may like to add an individual touch by having personalised cupcakes or maybe immortalising you and your partner on top of the cake (*see box above*). Meet with at least three designers, explain your thoughts and listen to their ideas. Get creative and make the wedding cake part of your day, not part of the furniture.

In the weddings we have helped to arrange, we have suggested:

WEB *link*. For more information on cake tops visit: http://www.pinkweddings.biz/goodies/caketops.htm

* Cutting the cake during the ceremony.
* Serving the wedding cake to your guests while the photographs are being taken.
* Cutting the cake at the evening celebration so everyone can enjoy a special moment.

CHOOSING YOUR FLOWERS

Flowers have always played an important part in opposite-sex weddings and for a Civil Partnership it's no different. Once known as a symbol of everlasting love, the flower represents happiness and conveys heart-felt emotions. The scent of a flower can add that extra touch to your day ... Well, as long as you don't suffer from hay fever.

Whichever flowers you decide on, be sure to find a florist that is happy to take time out to talk to you about the vast range of flowers and plants available to you (real and artificial). You ideally want someone who is interested in both of you and wants to find out which style of flower would best suit you and your partner on this special day. This may take time to find and decide on, so don't be rushed (see TOP tip).

TOP tip

If you live in Norwich but are holding your Civil Partnership in King's Lynn, contact at least three local florists in the King's Lynn area for prices and ideas.

Do your research

Find out more about the kind of flowers and designs you can have by speaking to established florists, (see *Directory of resources, pages 120–123*). Your local florist is always a great place to start. They should be able to offer you sound advice and give you ideas of what's suitable and within your budget. Most florists have examples of the kinds of flowers they suggest and also have albums with photographs of past wedding and venue work they have done. Have a look at all of these things to gauge how the flowers look, how good the designs are and the combinations of flowers that work.

Being green

Another great consideration for many couples today is the environment. Many are choosing to have 'green' or environmentally friendly weddings. In terms of flowers,

this may lead you to ask about locally sourcing your
flowers, or even buying or hiring plant displays rather
than using cut flowers. Another option, which is
becoming more popular with florists supplying opposite-
sex weddings, is the use of very high-quality fake flowers
and plants. Whatever you choose to do, it might also be
a nice gesture to donate your displays to local hospices,
hospitals or other charitable organisations.

Old favourites ... and new

Lilies and roses still prove very popular at any time of
the year. On the other hand, you may be looking for
something unusual that might add that extra touch of
class or might represent something meaningful, such as
the colours of our 'rainbow flag'. In the latter case, the
new and ever so popular rainbow rose would fit the bill.
The rose petals are naturally dyed through a special
process that controls how much colour reaches each
petal. The rose suddenly blooms into the colours of a
rainbow with spectacular results.

The following are particularly popular flowers:

Stephanotis is a Jasmine-scented flower. One of the
most popular wedding flowers, its name comes from
the Greek *stephanos*, which means 'crown', and *otos*,
which means 'ear': the five, earlike appendages link to
the staminal crown at the flower's centre. It has white,
waxy blooms, which omit a rich scent that will have
your guests' heads turning in appreciation.

Tuberoses are sweet-smelling white flowers, often used
in perfume and luxury toiletries. This flower is a great
talking point as it is both magical and mythical: its scent
is supposed to have special powers that empowers those
who inhale it. Try adding some crystals to enhance its

powers. Tuberoses are particularly great for creating that quintessentially British, outdoor country-garden-feel at wedding ceremonies.

Peonies are a very popular wedding flower. They appear in a variety of colours from soft pastels to vibrant reds, yellows and orange and offer a fresh, delicate scent that is similar but lighter than that of a rose. Some florists may try and steer you away from this flower, stating that they may not last, especially in a hand-held bouquet as the flower heads are heavy and the stems fine, but any good florist can wire the stem to make it more stable.

Any of the above flowers can be mixed together but we would recommend staying with no more than two flowers and some lovely deep green foliage for the backdrop of your hand-held bouquet. Don't forget to follow this look through to your table centrepieces and pedestals.

Colours

Choosing a colour theme can sometimes be easier than you think: ask yourselves what your favourite colours are and see if combining them works. Mike and I love orange and blue, but we also like pink and purple so we decided to use the latter combination as our colour theme in the overall look of our room when we had our Civil Partnership – right down to our button holes.

Mike and I recall the time when we spoke to a celebrity couple that had a love of red tulips. Even though these were out of season, we arranged to have a bouquet of 24 specially shipped over from the Netherlands. The couple were overjoyed at the display and surprised we made it happen – and all for a cost of £120.

TOP *tip*

Remember when going with white flowers to choose a prominent colour to add that wow-factor. Sometimes just one coloured flower can set a stir amongst all the white.

CHOOSING YOUR PHOTOGRAPHER

Because your Civil Partnership will be one of the most memorable days of your life, great care should be taken when choosing a photographer.

Take time to see several before making your choice and make sure they are happy to take the style of pictures you want and not just what that particular photographer would like. Ask to view portfolios that include at least one complete wedding, not just an album of 'best pictures' from several weddings. Make sure the photographs are sharp, well composed, everyone is looking at the camera and there are no distractions in the background. Most reputable photographers also have portfolios on their websites that can help you shortlist those you prefer.

Price

Prices vary considerably and the old adage 'you get what you pay for' is not always true. For instance, a photographer with business premises will more often than not charge more than a photographer working from home because of his or her overheads.

Most photographers offer various packages. Don't be afraid to ask if the packages can be tailored to suit your personal requirements and budget. Don't forget to use your checklist (*see pages 110–113*) and note down the photographers you would most like to meet; shortlist three ideally.

In 2008, Mike and I put together a survey to find out how much couples were prepared to spend on photographs of their day and 35 percent said between £300 to £600 with 29 percent prepared to pay around £1,500.

When your day is over and your honeymoon is but a distant memory, your photographs are crucial to help you remember the day. Make sure the photographer offers a good and diverse range of albums as part of your package or otherwise negotiate a price for just the photographs and buy your own direct. There are a lot of options, but we would also recommend looking at digital options as well.

Wedding albums

Everyone likes to capture special occasions and moments in photographs and on video or DVD. Wedding photographers and videographers usually arrange with couples to cover every aspect of the day, from the morning preparations through to the evening celebrations and the couple's escape. You can find out how best to choose the videographer that is right for you on pages 89–91.

Traditionally, photographs, CDs and DVDs are presented to the couple in a luxury wedding album. Many suppliers use a classic black or white range. We have discovered, through organising so many weddings, a couple of trends that offer a fresh way to present not just Civil Partnership images, but photographs from many other special occasions, as well.

An often-asked question is: *Can we have an album that complements our wedding theme?* Pink Weddings™ Ltd inspired a respected UK-based luxury-album manufacturer, Spicer Hallfield Ltd, to produce a range of wedding albums that broke away from the accepted

WEB *link*

To see the full Fierté™ range please visit:

http://www.fierte.co.uk

norms. This is the Fierté™ range (from the French word for 'Pride'), which includes albums in an explosion of colours (*see* WEB*link*). It is both fresh and contemporary and allows couples to match a colour theme used on their day (*see box below*).

Another trend that is challenging the traditional wedding album, as a memento of the day, has come about through the digital age and the increased use of digital cameras, websites and social networks such as MySpace and Facebook. These enable people to quickly and easily share images of their happy day with their loved ones and, also, if they want, complete strangers!

Today, many more couples are looking to have their wedding pictures and film provided in a digital way. Fear not! Digital albums like the Fierté™ range give couples a way to store CDs and DVDs in something that is a far more special than just an ordinary CD or DVD case.

Your day in your pocket

Digital memories can now be kept in a Fierté iAlbum™ which is fashionably styled to neatly hold Apple's iPod Nano™ in an album that looks and feels as special as the day was.

The range unfolds into five fantastic colours, from calm lilac to sky blue, the zesty orange with a pastel green or the ever-faithful soft pink, all moulded in a luxurious non-leather, feel-good pocket book.

Available online for only £29.99 this exclusive iAlbum has already caused a stir in the wedding market and changed the way some photographers look at presenting the whole package for the couple, their family and friends.
(*For the full range see* WEB*link*.)

It doesn't stop there, however. A growing number of couples (Mike and I included) prefer to keep photographs and movies on iPods™. This means photographs, moving images and even music memories of the day can be carried around with you and may even be shown on a TV or computer with the right software and equipment.

Key questions to ask

Remember one of the main suppliers for your day is the photographer so make sure you feel comfortable and are able to work closely with them when talking about what you're after: no one wants a bossy, obtrusive photographer.

In order to do this, ask questions right from the start. The following may help:

- Do you offer set packages?
- If so, what do they include and can we mix and match between the various packages?
- Will we receive a CD, DVD or the negatives?
- Are you the photographer who will be covering our wedding? If not, may we view that photographer's work and meet him or her before the day?
- Have you worked at our venue before? If not, will you visit it prior to our day?
- Are there any hidden charges we should know about? Does your price include VAT?
- How long will it be before we receive our proof album?
- What kind of albums and options are available for our photographs?
- Do you have backup equipment in case of malfunction or breakage?

* Do you offer digital only options?
* Traditionally a photographer only really covers the bride's preparations, what provision do you make for same-sex couples? Are both parties' preparations covered, if required?
* We are having two aisles (*see pages 57–59*), how will you cover this?

Civil Partnership-friendly photographers

WEB *link*.
Visit one of our recommended photographers at:
http://www.andywebbphotography.com

Check photographers' websites to see how compliant they are in offering opposite- and same-sex weddings. Enquiry forms should not list the 'Bride and Groom's' names, for example. The Equality Act (2007) was put into place to change attitudes in the retail and goods sector, for this purpose.

A close friend of ours, Andy Webb (*see* WEB*link*), wanted to be sure he offered a website that was fully inclusive, presented pictures of opposite- and same-sex couples at prices that suited anyone's budget.

Andy's booking form asks for 'your name and your partner's name' taking away the chance of upsetting any couple, while the words 'when planning your marriage or Civil Partnership' reflect a modern approach. This in our opinion is the way forward, in an era when suppliers must recognise the changing and better climate.

CHOOSING YOUR VIDEOGRAPHER

Wedding videographers have come a long way since the days of one camera operator with a large and obtrusive video camera. These days, you will find a huge array of companies, each with different studio equipment and editing techniques. That's why it's important to make sure you spend valuable time researching and comparing suppliers (see pages 76–77) until you find the right company for you and your partner (see TOP tip). Don't worry about the expense: a reputable videographer will help advise you what is practical and possible within your budget.

Every couple and each Civil Partnership is different, so whether you prefer stylishly edited work, an atmospheric cinematic look or contemporary effects, make sure you get a feel of what is out there before you take the plunge and don't dismiss suppliers that you feel do a great job but haven't done any Civil Partnerships before. Just explain what you are looking for and go from there.

When choosing a videographer, your first priority should be checking their portfolios. Most have these online or will happily send you a DVD to watch, if you ask. Always bear in mind that montage demos will show the very best clips and a good videographer will be proud to show off recent work too, so don't be afraid to ask to see a film of a full wedding to get a feel for their work. Remember when you're watching it that, like photography, the end result should be something you want to see again and again and also something that you can proudly show to generations to come.

TOP *tip*

We recommend getting at least three quotes and seeing how the videographers' services and prices match. Get a full price that includes filming, any music licensing and editing. You will probably need to set aside at least £1,500, including VAT.

WEB *link.*

Visit one of our recommended videographers at:

http://www.fxfilms.co.uk

The gang at FX Films (*see* WEB*link*) have a clear and fresh approach to filming. They take time to listen to you, understand what you want, especially if your Civil Partnership has a particular theme or idea behind it, and give advice on the style and approach that can best capture your day.

Ask the right questions, get the right person

Sometimes knowing the right questions to ask suppliers can help you get the best out of people. To help you do this, we have put together a concise list that should help you when you first make that important call:

- What format will you be able to offer? (For example, High-Definition Widescreen, or Standard Definition?)
- How many hours will you be filming for at my Civil Partnership?
- Do you offer a multi-camera option, for extra angles of the ceremony and possible speeches?
- Can I choose my own music to include in the final DVD?
- How long will it take for you to edit our day?
- How many copies are included in the price?

Some companies offer additions to their main wedding packages. 'Highlight Clips' are perfect if you'd like a 3- to 5-minute montage of your wedding to keep on a DVD, iPod™ or Webpage.

Something I know goes down really well is the idea of creating your very own 'love story' documentary, where you and your partner get to feel like film stars. It starts with the videographers interviewing you both in a relaxed and informal way, perhaps as you start to plan your Civil Partnership. It is a chance for you to share some loving memories, including moments such as when you first met and a few stories leading up to your Civil Partnership. A really nice touch is arranging to be interviewed separately so when you come to watch your special day weeks later, you both have some surprises. If your budget permits, the crew could also film a few close friends or family telling other little anecdotes, jokes or just passing on their love and best wishes – something you will always remember. Another alternative is to have a video booth (*see* TOP *tip*).

During the day of your Civil Partnership, the documentary could build on the excitement of the preparations by capturing the magic of your ceremony and the exuberance of the evening celebrations. At the end of the day, your videographer will edit all the footage into your special documentary – one, which you will be able to watch and enjoy with each other, perhaps on anniversaries, and with friends and family whenever you want.

Mike's favourite style of Civil Partnership footage is the 'Music Video'. You choose one or two songs or pieces of music that you both love and then discuss with your filmmaker how you can either mock up a pop video or better still storyboard your own. You can pick your cast from family and friends and brief them on the segments in which you would like them to appear. One couple we remember very well recreated with their guests the group dance from Michael Jackson's iconic 'Thriller' video and with the twist that it was set to ABBA's 'Dancing Queen' instead.

At the end of the day no matter what you decide on, get plenty of ideas and feedback, then sit down and decide together exactly what you want.

TOP *tip*

Consider having a video booth at your wedding and invite your loved ones to provide intimate and touching messages or to answer pre-arranged questions from you. This will provide you with some extra special memories of the day.

YOUR WEDDING RINGS

Choosing your wedding rings can be another stressful process. *Where do you start? How much should you spend? What's fashionable and what's not? Where do you begin to look?*

TOP *tip*

Titanium has become one of the most popular options for wedding rings because it's hard wearing and can be fashioned into modern and attractive jewellery.

Many couples still opt for the standard, stylish and traditional gold wedding bands, but there are a growing number that look for something a little different to celebrate their Civil Partnership. In such cases, the options are still endless. Mike and I are seeing increasing numbers of couples ask for contemporary and modern designs, including handmade rings, which ultimately offer that chic and, on occasion, completely unique finishing touch to your day (*see* TOP *tip*).

Make them come to you!

If you enjoy perusing the shops or are internet-savvy and enjoy and have the time to research your perfect ring, that's fine, but another way of finding that perfect ring is to invite a designer to come to see you in your home. This is a great way of seeing a complete selection of rings, of all descriptions – every metal, stone, type of diamond and so on – but in the comfort and safety of your own home. This means you will be relaxed, you won't feel under pressure or rushed to buy something within set store opening hours or because you're rushing to get back to work, and you can try on as many rings as you want, while relaxing with the people that care.

This arrangement may also prove more economical for you: for instance, Bliss Rings do not have shop premises and this is reflected in the price of their rings. Their staff like to have fun, enjoy their time with you and ensure you get exactly what you want; they stay for as long as you need them to and it's all for free ... well, except for the price of the rings.

Our own experience

When Mike and I looked for our rings we found a fantastic website called Love and Pride (see WEB*link*). They are committed to the gay and lesbian community, offering original and classic rings created by quality craftsman. Based in the United States, I thought it would be expensive to buy and ship rings back to the UK, but actually found out that prices were very reasonable – from only £50 upwards depending on the style. We were also really pleased to find out that Love and Pride donate 10 percent of their net proceeds to organisations that are committed to equal rights and marriage equality for gay and lesbian couples. One thing to bear in mind is that you may incur customs tax and duty on rings sent over from the United States.

Mike wanted his ring to reflect his balanced character so we went for a sleek Titanium design with a striking diamond, floating in the centre of a rectangular opening while mine broke away from the norm with a diamond set in the centre of the ring directly underneath its rectangular opening. So, when we show them off to people, they look like a pair but they also demonstrate our own individuality.

Other options

For those of you who don't like standard metals, are allergic to precious metals or are wanting something a little bit different and more natural, what would you say to wood?

When we first met Sandra, we discovered she was allergic to metal and she was frustrated as she felt that

WEB *link*

For a fantastic choice of rings visit:
http://www.loveandpride.com
For a more economical choice see:
http://www.blissrings.co.uk

WEB *link*

For a great selection of handmade wooden rings visit:
http://www.touchwoodrings.com

she had little or no choice of a ring for her Civil Partnership. We found a great range of handmade wooden rings (*see* WEB*link*), crafted using three thin slices of hardwoods bonded together to create a beautiful strong ring. It was extremely unusual, not to mention eco-friendly! These rings are a great alternative choice and start from only £60 upwards.

Over the years early records have shown that iron, steel, silver, copper, brass and even leather have been used as wedding rings. Today, the choice available to you is even larger so do take your time when looking. Try to get pictures of ones that you like and remember, if you're having something designed, it may take a while, so please plan ahead. These rings will help demonstrate your love and commitment to each other in front of your family and friends.

If rings are not for you, you can always try a different token to symbolise your commitment to each other. Some couples exchange bracelets as a sign of their love for one another. One couple we know, actually gave each other key rings holding keys to new cars!

WHAT TO WEAR

Some people have dreamed about their wedding since they were children, mapping out exactly what they would wear on their special day. To most of us, however, choosing an outfit can be the most daunting of tasks. *Where do you start? What should you wear? What's acceptable and what's not?* Commonly, many men question if they should wear a traditional top hat and tails or go down another route. Women, on the other hand, may worry over whether to wear a white wedding dress or something altogether different. An added worry is what to dress your best team in.

Mike and I have seen so many changes in fashion and trends over the last six years and some fantastic new ideas and concepts have emerged. This section is just about giving you some personal pointers and revealing some of our favourite designers.

From personal experience

For our special day, Mike and I had our suits designed by Gresham Blake (*see* WEB*link*), a fantastic designer, who has created outfits for the likes of David Bowie and Davina McCall. We asked Gresham for something a little bit different that would also incorporate our chosen colour theme – Pink and Purple. After much consultation, Mike and I finally settled on a stylish black pinstripe suit with the stripe in purple. Mike wore the jacket, waistcoat, trousers and purple shirt with matching tie and black shoes, while I wore the jacket and trousers, spat shoes and a pink shirt with no waistcoat and no tie. While our suits were identical, the way in which we chose to accessorise them brought out our two personalities, as well as tying in perfectly with our chosen theme (*see* TOP *tip*).

WEB *link*

To view Gresham Blake's designs visit:
http://www.greshamblake.com

TOP *tip*

If you both choose to wear the same suit, by alternating the colour of your suits and shirts, you can create a look that is both stylish and breaks with tradition slightly.

Gresham Blake has showrooms in Brighton and London in England; he offers a bespoke service and an off-the-peg range and also now has a celebrity range with designs by comedian Matt Lucas, cultural commentator Jonathan Ross and musician The Edge, among others.

Our recommendations

Through Pink Weddings™, we recommend many people who we have worked with and with whom we have trusted relationships.

Men

We have worked with Anthony's for many years, whose venture A Civil Affair (*see* WEB*link*) offers stylish, coloured suits for men, from the UK and Europe. Antony's produces both traditional wear and suits with a bit of pizzazz, in such colours as burnt orange, lilac, lime, ivory and burgundy. Colour can add that extra fantastic wow-factor, particularly if it ties in with your chosen colour theme, as it did on our day.

Women

We have helped a number of our couples wanting to have a Civil Partnership overcome concerns about feeling uncomfortable when approaching local bridal shops and trying on dresses in public by simply making private appointments (*see* TOP *tip*). There are many formal and bridal wear retailers who are happy to help in such circumstances (*see Directory of resources, pages 120–123*).

In 2008 we ran a survey on our website asking women what they would wear to their Civil Partnership. Over 44 percent said they would prefer to wear a dress.

If the idea of wearing a white wedding dress scares the living daylights out of you, have a look online at some

> **TOP *tip***
>
> *If you feel any concern about approaching bridal shops it's best to call first and say you're planning your Civil Partnership to get a feel for their reaction.*

stylish evening or formal dresses such as those found in the Wedding Shop's bridesmaids area (*see* WEB*link*) that you can either have customised or accessorise to add that little extra sparkle.

A close second on our survey was for ladies to wear suits. A stylish suit mixing shirts with a skirt or pair of trousers can create an elegant touch that easily replaces the wedding dress, but retains the impact. Our friends, Debbie and Elaine Gaston, wore beautiful white, high-collared suits and held matching floral bouquets with pink roses. Debbie is also a reverend and wore a lovely pink shirt with a white dog collar for that personal touch.

Themes

Some couples base their wedding attire on a mutually chosen theme to make a statement or just make their

WEB*link*

For the perfect dress visit:
http://www.theweddingsinzp.co.uk/bridesmaids.html
For stylish mens' suits visit:
http://www.acivilaffair.cc.uk
For fabulous kilts visit:
http://www.masterkiltmaker.com

Kilts for both sexes

One of the fastest growing outfits of choice at the moment is the kilt, worn by both men and women. One company particularly close to us is the Master Kilt Maker (*see* WEB*link*).

When speaking to the gang there, it's amazing what options they have to offer you and your partner: the list is endless and it doesn't stop at just the kilt itself. To make the overall look even more spectacular, they can include a sash, sporran, decorative pins and kilt jackets.

You may want to find your own family tartan to wear, but if you can't, how about a kilt made from the country you are from, or a particular region that you love. Examples might be the Welsh National Tartan, Tartan of Holland, Spanish Shirt or Chinese Scottish, to name but a few.

Something old, something new ...

Phil and Brian, who have been together for 23 years, decided to follow a tradition usually associated with opposite-sex weddings. They wore their most comfortable and well-worn shoes ('something old'), with engraved watches ('something new'), their best friends' cufflinks ('something borrowed') and each of them wore a blue garter ('the something blue') that none of us saw – until later in the evening, that is!

day more special. Take someone you either love or loathe – Kitten, the rebellious housemate from the UK reality TV show *Big Brother* (2005), and her partner chose a 'rags to riches' theme. Kitten wore ripped jeans complete with top hat and tails, while her partner wore a sequinned dress in beige. At the other end of the spectrum, a lovely couple, whose Partnership we arranged, chose our 'Bollyrouge™' theme, which incorporates elements of Bollywood glamour and Arabic flair with the excitement and flamboyance of the Moulin Rouge in Paris. They chose to wear saris and the rich gold and reds of flowing silk combined with the feathered fronds, which were carried through by Pink Weddings™ to the Bedouin-style tents, merged some of the traditions of India and the Arab world with the decadence of France.

Be comfortable

Whatever you and your partner decide to wear make sure you feel comfortable wearing it and don't be pressured into a design or style with which you're not happy. It's your special day and you must both wear whatever makes you happy.

Transport

Increasingly, couples are looking to turn up to their ceremony or celebration not just in style but also in something different. So it is not always about using the traditional vintage or luxury car; sometimes it is about adding an early wow-factor to your day.

When you look for transport, it is amazing what you can find, from the stretched-mini limo to funky, matching VW Beetles. One option close to Mike's heart is arriving on a sunny day in Morris Minor convertibles, but for me it has to be arriving in a chauffeured supercar like a Lamborghini – probably my Italian roots shining through! (*See* TOP *tip for some more unusual ideas.*)

One couple we recall, decided to ferry themselves and their guests in a fleet of cars. Jeff and Neil were in a beautiful Bentley Continental while their best team arrived in many different luxury cars that included a Porsche, Lotus Elise, Jaguar E-type, TVR, BMW Z3 and Mazda RX8. I have to say the line up was not just amazing but impressive as they turned up ready for their day. But be warned – these types of vehicles do come at a price.

You may also like to consider arranging transportation between locations for your best team and VIP guests. Karen and Dianne wanted to start the celebrations on the way from their ceremony to their reception venue and so they decided to use the fabulous Blush Disco pink London doubledecker bus (*see* WEB*link*). Its stunning interior and high technology entertainment equipment gave their guests a ride they will probably never forget.

TOP *tip*

At Pink Weddings™ we have even turned a Ferrari pink for one couple's day. Not often seen, in fact hardly ever, but a jaw dropper for sure, it certainly introduced their colour theme to guests. Car fans don't panic: the Ferrari was returned to its factory colour without any damage.

WEB *link*

For more information on the Blush Disco bus visit:

http://www.blush-hospitality.com

WEDDING GIFT LISTS

Wedding gift lists have been a part of opposite-sex couples' wedding arrangements for years. It is also something that has become popular with same-sex couples, but if you have owned or rented your own property or have lived together as a couple for a while, the chances are you probably have all the things traditionally put on a wedding list. Some people claim that the reign of the traditional gift list is over and that the endless stream of toasters and towels should be buried. Mike would agree with this, but I believe that there is a place for them still. Whatever your thoughts, it is always good to know what is available out there and how to select the right company and list for you and your partner.

Loved ones quite often want to give you a present when you hold your Civil Partnership. It may be something you already have or something simply not to your taste, and that in itself is a huge waste of money and time, as well as embarrassing if you want to return it or end up having to live with something you hate. A wedding list gives you the opportunity to decide exactly what you need or desire. It can be practical, aspirational – or both – and could range from something as basic as a kettle to donating money to your favourite charity or receiving contributions towards your perfect honeymoon or even a car. It is a great way for you and your partner to get all the essentials for setting up home for the first time or, for example, to replace cutlery you already have with a much-desired Georg Jensen service.

It is also a way to take the pressure off your guests and also off your best team, who otherwise have to deal with wrapped bulky or fragile presents on the day.

Another nice feature of many gift lists is that several people can club together and each contribute an amount towards an expensive item, which they know you both desire.

So where do you start? Almost every high-street chain and department store offers a gift list service and if you add in online providers, the choice is enormous.

Here are some tips on how best to proceed:

- Firstly, you and your partner should discuss what kind of gifts you would like.
- If you already have everything you need, think creatively. For example, you could set up a special account to which people could contribute and use that to help pay off your mortgage once and for all, or redesign your home or professionally landscape your garden.
- Then start researching companies: asking friends and family for their recommendations is a good idea, similarly looking at books such as this one, consumer magazines and guides will help.

Wedding Gift Options
We have listed below some ideas and options available to you:

Department stores
Having a wedding gift list with a department store is popular with many people simply because they are likely to have the variety of products you need at a range of prices to suit most of your loved ones' pockets.

Many, like John Lewis, Harvey Nichols and Debenhams, have branches around the country and offer online

John Lewis, top of the game

Over the years working with reputable suppliers and a diverse number of happy couples, Mike and I have seen five styles of gift list provider bubble to the top in popularity.

In the 2008 survey commissioned and conducted by Pink Weddings™, the department store, John Lewis, was the public's number one choice followed by The Alternative Gift List and the department store Selfridges, in third place.

John Lewis has always been supportive of Civil Partnerships and offers a great choice for same-sex couples. Its brand and the level of service provided reflects the company's modern and stylish approach.

services, which are great if guests live in different parts of the UK, or even abroad. Although some people think that department stores don't offer the service or personality of smaller or more specialist wedding list companies, in a recent survey the retail group John Lewis came out top with customers (*see box above*).

Charity donations

We are starting to see couples turning to alternative lists that ask their guests to donate money to charity, help developing countries or even adopt animals on the couple's behalf. This is a way for established couples or those with a philanthropic bent to help support causes they care about.

Our friends at The Alternative Gift List (*see* WEB*link*), for example, offer couples the chance to create wedding gift lists based on donating money to a charity that they feel strongly about. All you have to do is choose a charity you would like to help and set up a 'wedding list', asking guests to support it by buying something

WEB *link.*
For more information on charity gift lists visit: http://www.thealternativegiftlist.co.uk

Here are a few examples of the difference you can make through charitable donations:

Breast Cancer Care

£10 offers one Headstrong session. Hair loss following treatment can be a devastating reminder of the impact breast cancer has on everyday life. A donation could enable one person to attend HeadStrong, providing emotional support and practical tips to people who are coping with hair loss after treatment, giving them vital confidence.

Mencap

£50 will help a person with a learning disability realise a dream. The donation could pay for a simulated flight, an art course or classes where that person can learn something new.

Terrance Higgins Trust (THT)

Among many other services, THT provides support groups for mothers and children with HIV. Many mothers and children living with HIV don't have anyone to talk to and can become very isolated. £100 could enable THT to hire a safe venue for five support groups, allowing mothers and their children to talk without fear about their concerns for the first time and receive the confidential advice they need.

that is important to the cause. Donations can range from as little as £10 up to £280, or more, depending on the generosity of your loved ones (*see box above for examples*).

Getaways or Honeymoon Gift Lists

Turning our minds to honeymoons – and we all get excited at the prospect of choosing a new country or destination for that special break to start our lives as legal partners – but on occasion the cost of the honeymoon can be prohibitive.

This is a way for you both to truly have a dream vacation or luxury trip you have longed for without spending all your well-earned savings and is a great way for guests to be involved in helping a couple get away on that ever so special honeymoon.

Co-op Travelcare has a great honeymoon gift list service, which allows you and your partner to book your honeymoon. You are given a reference number, which can easily be included when sending out the invitations for your day. Guests simply call in with this number and they can pay as much or as little as they like towards your honeymoon.

Online

With nearly everyone, including those friends and families overseas, having access to the internet and World Wide Web these days, online specialists are a convenient way to manage a gift list.

TheGiftListCompany.com gives you the freedom of choice to source products from any retailer, including expensive gifts that guests can contribute an amount towards. You can create and manage your gift list at your leisure, then TheGiftListCompany.com will discreetly invite your guests to choose a gift you'll love and transfer them to the retailer to make their purchase directly.

TOP *tip*

Credit card payments are probably the safest way to ensure that if the worst happens, you will be entitled to a refund, but double check with your card company before making any purchases to see if you are covered.

As with anything online, you should investigate a company's credentials carefully and be confident that they are legitimate before signing up. One major online gift list company went into administration in 2007 and caused widespread concern about what happens to funds and gifts that have been purchased, but have yet to be delivered. You should remember to always ask the supplier what protection they can offer should things go pear-shaped (*see* TOP *tip*).

Do it yourself

It may take a little more planning, however, if you
cannot bring yourself to use a gift list service and you
would prefer to have something more personal – an
alternative is for you to create your own!

For years, we have worked alongside Mary, editor of
Wedding Professional magazine. She told us of one couple
who sent out paying-in slips from their bank with their
invitations. It certainly did the job – if not in the most
subtle of ways.

One couple we remember chose another, perhaps more
interactive, way of getting what they most desired. Sue
and Rebecca wanted to have a garden makeover. With
the help of a landscaper they created the garden of their
dreams and then broke it down into gift-sized elements.
Their personal wedding gift list consisted of things like
a new deck, a water feature and new plants all listed
individually. Friends and family then contributed
towards the whole garden!

A nice touch, which Mike and I suggested, was to
include a name plate with the details of the giver in
areas of their garden and on key features like seating,
as a reminder for Sue and Rebecca and a thank you
for the presents.

No matter what style of gift list you decide on, be
sure to get the very best out of the service and take
away as much of the stress as possible and just enjoy
the planning.

TOP *tip*

A great way to start the evening off with a bang is to suspend two giant exploding balloons above the dance floor. These balloons can be filled with miniature balloons, feathers and glitter. When the balloons explode the music begins and you will find people will hit the dance floor early on in the evening and the children love playing with all the little balloons released. (see Directory of resources, pages 120–123)

ENTERTAINMENT

It has been our experience that compared with many opposite-sex weddings, same-sex couples put greater emphasis on entertainment for both their guests and themselves. When planning your evening reception, for example, you do not have to simply have the venue's DJ playing while a hot or cold buffet is served from uninspiring white-clothed tables. More and more couples are asking us to help find them that added touch, idea or wow-factor for their evening reception that will complement the day's events, as well as providing evening guests with a memorable time (*see* TOP *tip*). Top on the list in 2008, for instance, was mixing a good-quality DJ with a live tribute band or act.

DJ

When looking for good entertainment, don't be pressured into a venue's house DJ just because it is 'included' in your overall package. Always ask to speak with the DJ to get an idea of what he or she offers, including such things as lighting equipment and the style of music before saying 'yes'. Look at some sample playlists from previous celebrations.

DJs have changed over the years and many provide a more personalised and bespoke service by tailoring the music to suit your individual tastes. A good DJ should also be expert at gauging what music will suit the specific arrangements of a couple's Civil Partnership on the night itself, always ensuring that the right atmosphere is created for what is often a mixture of age groups and backgrounds. I think almost everyone of us knows from experience that having the right discotheque ambience really can make all the difference in the world to a wedding.

Typically, the disco will amount to roughly half of the overall time your guests will spend at your wedding reception. However, it is bizarrely often just a small fraction of the overall budget for a wedding. In our opinion, for couples looking at making the most of their evening's entertainment, it is certainly worth spending that little bit extra time and money to find and engage an excellent DJ because it is one of the main things that 'makes' your evening.

Playlists

There really is no excuse for a good DJ to have a small or single-genre music collection for you to choose from. Be sure to ask the DJ what kind of playlist he or she has; good DJs will be able to create a playlist that covers a wide range of music for both you and your guests.

For six years now, Tom Ryder (*see* WEB*link*) has looked after many same-sex couples' evening disco for us on their special day. Tom uses the very latest, state of the art audio and lighting equipment to ensure you enjoy the very best sound quality and atmosphere possible. Now, turning to look at budgeting for this – don't be surprised if you are quoted around £700 upwards. You can get a great package for around £400, but check exactly what's included for that price.

Tribute acts

Tribute acts are a relatively new and fast growing phenomena at Civil Partnership celebrations. Imagine the added wow-factor in your ceremony or celebration when a look-a-like of your favourite performer shows up. Once upon a time, tribute bands recreated the sounds and looks of acts who no longer perform; such as The Beatles, ABBA and Queen; but these days as soon as a new band or singer emerges onto the scene

TOP *tip*

Let your DJ know if you have live acts in the programme and have them ease the transition from live sets to disco and vice versa via the use of their PA systems.

WEB *link*

For more information on DJ Tom Ryder visit:
http://www.musicforoccasion.com

WEB *link*

Our little performer, Life of Kylie, is a fantastic tribute act, visit her myspace site to hear more: http://www.myspace.com/lifeofkylie

a tribute act follows very closely behind. This opens up the choice and gives you the chance to engage tributes to the likes of Madonna, Cher, Kylie (*see* WEB*link*), Robbie and even Justin Timberlake, to name but a few. These heart-pumping, feet-tapping performers really know how to get a party going.

Mike and I remember arranging a cowboy-western themed wedding and the two guys wanted this to somehow carry through into the evening's party. We arranged for a Dolly Parton tribute act to meet and greet guests and then perform some good old-fashioned country anthems. Unexpectedly, we also persuaded a local line-dancing group to lead the couple and guests in a little dosie doe.

Live bands and acts

A live act or band can have a place throughout the day and evening: during the ceremony itself providing background music, keeping guests entertained while photographs are being taken, right down to the evening bash. The list is so extensive these days that you are sure to find an act that will deliver what you require, from medieval flutes and chants to smooth vocals and jazz.

Whomever you finally decide on, don't forget to get your hands on their CD first or, better still, why not go with your partner to hear them play live as a treat during your planning? Sometimes seeing, hearing and feeling a performance will give you the best chance to understand how they will fit into your Civil Partnership.

Also bear in mind the drag queen, who may be acting as your master of ceremony for the occasion. She may provide all manner of entertainment, from stand-up to cabaret (*see Toastmaster … or drag queen, pages 62–64*).

Chapter 4

MAKING THE DAY HAPPEN

'There is only one happiness in life, to love and be loved.'

– GEORGE SAND, WRITER

YOUR CIVIL PARTNERSHIP CHECKLISTS

Now no one ever said it would be easy planning your Civil Partnership, but many couples fail to realise how much time it can take, not to mention the stress it can cause. It may seem over the top to create a detailed checklists but as the months, weeks and days go by it may not seem so crazy, after all. In addition, creating, using and updating your checklist will also help you to keep an eye on your budget.

Your 12-month checklist:

1. Announce your engagement.
2. Hire a wedding planner/consultant, if you feel you need a helping hand.
3. Set a date to give notice of your Civil Partnership ceremony (*see pages 17–20*).
4. Have you considered a prenup (*see page 21*)?
5. Consider the financial and legal implications of a Civil Partnership (*see pages 22–27*).
6. Decide if you or your partner are going to change your names (*see pages 29–30*).
7. Choose a date and time (*see pages 37–38*).
8. Send out your 'save the date' cards and choose your invitations (*see pages 39–41*).
9. Decide on the kind of signing and ceremony you would like (*see pages 42–45*).
10. Research venues and check availability; reserve this if you're able to (*see pages 46–48*).
11. Book the venue once your date is confirmed.
12. Decide on your best team (*see pages 52–55*).
13. Research a drag queen or toastmaster, if required; check availability/book (*see pages 62–64*).

14.   Set a wedding budget (*see pages 70–74*).

15.   Does the venue provide the meal? What are your options? If not, find a caterer (*see pages 78–79*).

16.   Find a selection of florists and arrange a meeting with at least three (*see pages 81–83*).

17.   Research the photographers and arrange to meet them (*see pages 84–88*).

18.   If you're planning to have a video of the day, get some DVDs and arrange to meet videographers that appealed to you (*see pages 89–91*).

19.   Research wedding ring designs (*see pages 92–94*)

20.   Start your search for what you and your best team will wear (*see pages 95–98*).

21.   Think about transport on the day (*see page 99*).

22.   Do you want a gift list? If so, look into your options and check ranges (*see pages 100–105*).

23.   Decide on the kind of music and entertainment for the day and evening (*see pages 106–108*).

24.   Visit the *Gay Wedding Show*™ for ideas to help planning your day.

25.   Make sure you have any contracts for suppliers you wish to book.

26.   Does the venue have accommodation they can hold for any guests wishing to stay over the period of your Civil Partnership?

Now everything is coming together, what's next?

Your 6- to 9-month checklist:

1.   Finalise your guest list for the day and evening and send out the invitations.

2.   Have you bought outfits for you and your partner plus the team?

3.   Start looking at destinations and costs for your honeymoon (*see pages 49–51*).

WEB *link*

For ideas, inspiration, information and more, visit the UK's official Gay Wedding Show™:
http://www.gayweddingshow.co.uk

4.   Book your photographer.
5.   Book your videographer (if you're having one).
6.   Book your florist.
7.   Book your DJ, tribute band or live band.
8.   Book your wedding car.
9.   Look into a wedding cake (*see pages 78–79*).

With most booking done and contracts signed, here are the final touches that will make your day amazing.

Your 4- to 6-month checklist:

1.   Decide on design and buy your rings.
2.   Order your wedding cake.
3.   Select your 'thank you' notes and stationery, and then order them.
4.   Send your Civil Partnership announcement to the newspaper (first gay couple appeared in the *Daily Telegraph* newspaper).

Crunch time is here and it's only 2 to 4 months before your big day!

Your 2- to 4-month checklist:

1.   Prepare maps and directions for the ceremony and reception.
2.   Buy your wedding guest book or tree.
3.   Finalise all bookings made in the first 12 months.
4.   Select gifts for your best team.
5.   Finalise transport.
6.   Finalise your menu for the reception.
7.   Purchase all wedding accessories.
8.   Arrange your seating plan (*see pages 60–61*).
9.   Prepare your seating cards.
10.   Finalise the music for your ceremony.

A few weeks left to go – you are now at the stage where everything should be done and only final little details and touches are needed:

1.   Make sure all clothing and accessories for you and the team are ready and fit comfortably.
2.   Review any seating details with your team.
3.   Pack for your honeymoon.
4.   Call any guests who have not responded.
5.   Wrap the wedding party gifts.

Keeping everyone organised

It may seem a waste of time to keep a record of what you or other people will be doing at every stage of planning. Without it, however, it becomes all too easy for something small but crucial to slip through the gap.

Having a spreadsheet outlining when things need to be done, who's doing it and if it's been actioned, will help keep things on track and allow you to be organised and in control. It is also a great way for you to keep on top of all the things you have asked your best team to do.

Mike's simple but useful 'Supplier Log' spreadsheet follows. You may care to use this as it is or modify it to cover your own requirements. You can annotate it as you start to get various essentials arranged.

As a thank you from us, you can download an Excel version of this log at www.pinkweddings.biz/yourday. Just use the password *thebook*.

We hope this will help make things run a little bit more smoothly and make things a little bit less stressful.

Enjoy your day!

FOR THE	SERVICE	NAME & CONTACT DETAILS (phone, email, emergency mobile)	COST	CONTRACT SIGNED OR CONFIRMED	DELIVERY EXPECTED	NOTES
run-up	outfits					
run-up	gift list					
run-up	event co-ordinator					
run-up	stationery					eg. save the date, invitatio
run-up	planner					
run-up	insurance					eg. wedding, public liabilit
run-up	venue					
day	accommodation – couple					
day	accommodation – guests					
ceremony	celebrant					
ceremony	themed decorations					eg. seat covers, lighting
ceremony	stationery					eg. ceremony booklets
ceremony	florist					eg. button holes, bouquets
ceremony	music					eg. harpist, singer
ceremony	photographer					
ceremony	readings					eg. Auntie Sue
ceremony	videographer					
ceremony	transportation					eg. limo, buses
ceremony	witnesses					eg. Jo and Tony
ceremony	rings or gift exchange					
celebration	balloons					
celebration	florist					eg. centrepieces, pedastals
celebration	catering					
celebration	gift/card handling					eg. best team
celebration	photographer					
celebration	guest book handling					
celebration	themed decorations					eg. seat covers/lighting
celebration	master of ceremonies					eg. drag act, toastmaster
celebration	videographer					
celebration	outdoor arrangements					eg. kitchen, marquee, toile
celebration	stationery					eg. name cards, seating pla
celebration	music/entertainment					e.g. DJ, band, tribute act
celebration	speeches					eg. Shaun, Nick
celebration	wedding cake					
celebration	fireworks					
celebration	transportation					
celebration	lighting					
celebration	entertainment					eg. live act, magician
celebration	bar					
celebration	power/electrical					eg. bouncy castle generato
afterwards	getaway or honeymoon					
afterwards	photography album					eg. Fierté™ album
afterwards	thank you notes/gifts					eg. best team
afterwards	collecting videos/dvds					

Chapter 5

THE DAY ITSELF

'Being deeply loved by someone gives you strength; loving someone deeply gives you courage.'

– LAO TZU, PHILOSOPHER

FINAL DETAILS AND ENJOYING YOUR DAY

The time has come to finalise everything and the last few moments are here before all you have planned and arranged for your day finally starts to become a reality – and the nerves kick in.

Mike and I know what it is like to go through the final details before leaving for our big day, back on that cold December morning in 2005. It was probably one of the most nerve-racking moments of our lives and definitely one of the most exciting too.

We know from experience that there is so much happening at that moment that it's difficult to remain calm and in control (see TOP tip). Remember that all your planning should now start to really pay-off. Also, remember that you have your best team. Make sure you use them to do what you have agreed with them!

Mike and I have jotted down a few little tips and tricks for you which we found great on our day and that our team now use with the couples Pink Weddings™ help.

TOP tip

When it's time to get spruced up and dressed for your day, take a moment alone for you and your partner. Share a glass of water or champagne, and savour the moment before the fun starts.

The checklist

Have your checklist with you (see pages 110–113) just to be sure and make sure your team has copies as well.

The room

It is easy to get wrapped up in the minute detail of such things as the theme preparations, table setting and room decoration. Remember the overall appearance and feel is much more important than tiny details. Mike almost filed for a dissolution before our Civil Partnership when

I produced a tape measure to see if all the table centrepieces were the same height for our reception! Hopefully, these are the points you have told your co-ordinator or best team to check anyway.

Once the ceremony or celebration room has been decorated, leave the room for about half an hour. After that, come back and look at the overall impact. It's like looking through a fresh pair of eyes and you should be wowed by the final look. Walk around just to reassure yourself that everything you have ordered on your Supplier Log (*see page 114*) is there and you're happy.

Getting dressed

First thing, perhaps when you get up after your breakfast cuppa, set out your outfits, accessories and shoes, ready for when you need to change. It is also the perfect time to check you have remembered everything in good enough time for you to do something about it if you have forgotten something. For one of our couples, Gerry and Dave on their special day, Mike was dispatched to get a pair of cufflinks, all part of being a wedding planner on the day!

Your best team

Almost everyone reacts differently on the day. Your best team each has his or her own role and you and your partner each have yours. Make sure everyone knows what's expected and thank your best team at the start of your day (*see* TOP *tip*) as well as during your speeches.

The rings and things

Who has got and who will hold the important items you'll need for your ceremony? Check you have essentials like your promises to each other and rings or gifts you will exchange. Doublecheck and then check those again!

TOP *tip*

For our day, we dropped off little pocket-sized cards with a few kind words and thanks to our best team: it's a lovely touch which reminds them just how much you care before the day has started.

Our experience

When I look back at our day, I remember butterflies were doing an Irish Jig in my stomach, while Mike seemed so cool, calm and collected. We were awoken in our suite at 5 a.m. with a light room-service breakfast and four different alarm calls, which made sure we woke up! Our morning was calm and quiet, giving Mike and me the chance to enjoy our breakfast. Our best team were told only to disturb us before 7 a.m. if there was an emergency.

Lo and behold, 7 a.m. arrived and our team were at the door, ready and excited. Before we knew it, champagne corks were flying and the mayhem had started. For the next 15 minutes it felt like organised chaos but ever so much fun.

The limo arrived at the Hilton Metropole at 7.15 a.m. and Mike, our best team, witnesses and I were all bundled in for our 5-minute drive to the register office. We hadn't anticipated that our route to Brighton's Town Hall would be blocked by various TV broadcast vans but it only took 11 minutes longer than planned and so we arrived fashionably late at 7.35 a.m.

On arrival, our best team started to make sure everything was ready. Meanwhile, Mike and I were free to face the world's

Keep wet

Stress and excitement will have a physical effect that may pop up and surprise you. Keep some water and small mints available. Aruna, our lush publisher, frowns on gratuitous sweet advertising so pick your favourite, and keep them handy throughout your day. Your partner, guests and, in fact, everyone knows it is always good to have fresh breath but you'll also find it helps keeps a dry mouth at bay (*see* TOP *tip*).

Keep dry

Waterworks at a wedding is a cliché that just keeps turning up. Mike and I have seen even the hardest,

TOP *tip*

Make sure there is a glass of water close by during your ceremony in case you, your partner or the celebrant need a sip while saying those all important words.

press as we made our way into the beautifully decorated register office. Before we even had time to realise what was happening it was close to 8 a.m. and Mike and I were in the ceremony room hearing a countdown to the very moment that Civil Partnerships became law in England. Trevor Love, our registrar and close friend, was getting us and our witnesses ready to sign the official register and we became one of the first couples in the UK to legally enter a Civil Partnership.

The ceremony that followed was beautiful and there was not a dry eye in the room. Suddenly it seemed we were outside in front of hundreds of well-wishers and more media. Our day had truly begun. The wedding breakfast was fun and literal – yes we really did have breakfast: hash browns, fried eggs, bacon and baked beans were all on the menu at 9 a.m. After speeches, interviews and present opening it was 2 p.m. and we were in our suite sipping champagne, the day was almost over.

I guess what Mike and I are trying to say is that no matter what you plan for your day, make sure you savour and enjoy every minute of it because before you know it the day is over. It's amazing how much time can be taken up planning this one special day only to have it zip past so fast but you will have some fantastic memories for years to come.

butchist, macho builders break down in tears, along with their wives, at a Civil Partnership. Maybe it is the emotion and genuine love that pours out or perhaps the joy at seeing their gay mates finally join them in a legally recognised union. Whatever the cause, make sure you remember to keep a pack of tissues at hand.

... And finally

Congratulations on your future Civil Partnership and welcome to your part in making history!

–love Gino and Mike

DIRECTORY OF RESOURCES

See Pink Weddings™ website for full listings.

CELEBRANTS/CEREMONIES

Alternative Ceremony
www.GayWeddingsInScotland.org

Civil Ceremonies Ltd
Nationwide Celebrants
www.civilceremonies.co.uk

Rainbow Heart Services Limited
www.rainbowheartservices.co.uk

Rev Debbie Gaston (Brightwaves MCC
Brighton)
www.mccbrighton.org.uk

CLOTHING

A Civil Affair
www.acivilaffair.co.uk

Brides & Grooms Ltd
Birmingham
www.groomsmenswear.co.uk

Divine Bridal
Nottinghamshire
www.divinebridal.com

Gresham Blake
Brighton
www.greshamblake.com

Moss Bros Group Plc
www.moss.co.uk

Pinkbutterflybrides
Bridalwear, Cardiff
www.pinkbutterflybrides.co.uk

Simply Brides of Didcot
Oxfordshire
www.SimplyBrides.net

The Master Kilt Maker
London
www.masterkiltmaker.com

The Wedding Shop
Essex
www.theweddingshop.co.uk

Well Groomed
London
www.wellgroomed-formalhire.co.uk

FOOD & DRINK

Bridal Cakes.
North Hampshire
www.bridalcakes.co.uk

Food Show Ltd
London
www.foodshow.org.uk

Jalapeno London
www.jalapenolondon.co.uk

Jilly Bean Cake Toppers
Cambridgeshire
www.jillybeans-cake-toppers.com

Kalm Kitchen
Surrey
www.kalmkitchen.co.uk

Lindas Pantry
West Sussex.
www.lindaspantry.co.uk

The Mobile Cocktail Company
Dorset
www.themobilecocktailcompany.co.uk

Pink Cakes
Kent
www.pinkcakes.co.uk

Sharon Walker
Wedding Cakes, West Sussex
www.sharonscakes.co.uk

DIRECTORIES

ChooseYourWedding.com
Somerset
www.chooseyourwedding.com

Gay to Z Directory
www.gaytoz.com/civilpartnerships.asp

The Pink Guide
www.thepinkguide.co.uk

Purple Unions
www.purpleunions.com

Weddingsday
Nationwide
www.weddingsday.co.uk

ENTERTAINMENT

ANONYMOUS – Venetian Statues
East London
www.anonimo.biz

Deal A Party.com
Cardiff
www.dealaparty.com

Dixie Tucker
Drag queen
www.dixitucker.co.uk

Fonda Cox
Drag queen, Brighton
www.fondacox.com

Gypsyfire
Gloucestershire
www.gypsyfire.co.uk

ISIS String Quartet
Birmingham
www.isisquartet.co.uk

Jo Paige
London
www.uniqueentertainments.com

Lee Warren Magician
London
www.leewarrenmagic.co.uk

Life of Kylie and Madonna
Tribute Act, Nationwide
www.myspace.com/lifeofkylie

Manchester Lesbian & Gay Chorus
Greater Manchester
www.mlgc.org.uk

Miss Direction - The Drag Magician
London
www.miss-direction.com

Music251
Nationwide
www.music251.com

Natural Theatre Company
Bath
www.naturaltheatre.co.uk

Paul Martin Magician
London
www.paulmartinmagic.com

Tom Ryder - DJ
www.musicforoccasion.com

Smooth Duo
Nottinghamshire
www.smoothduo.co.uk

StarTurn
London
www.starturn.biz

Steve Dela Magic
London
www.stevedela.com

Video Guestbook & Bespoke Disco
Cardiff
www.uniqueparties.co.uk

Vintage Music (Whatsyatag Ltd)
Nationwide
www.whatsyatag.com

Graham West
Harpist, Canterbury
www.grahamwestharpist.co.uk

EVENT DECORATION
Enchanting Tables and Chairs
Cardiff
www.enchantingtablesandchairs.co.uk

Lavenders of London
Nationwide
www.lavendersoflondon.com

Renaissance Creative Design Ltd
Brighton
www.renaissancecreativedesign.co.uk

Reveries
West Sussex
www.reveriesweddings.co.uk

Wedding Planner Wales
www.weddingplannerwales.com

FLORISTS
Fleur de Paris
www.fleur-de-paris.co.uk

Florian
Brighton
www.flowers-brighton-hove.co.uk

Flowerworks
Gloucester
www.flowerworksuk.com

Frog Flowers
Greater Manchester
www.frogflowers.co.uk

The Divine Flower Company
Middlesex
www.divine-flowers.co.uk

Village Flower Studio
Rumney
www.villageflowerstudio.com

GIFT LISTS
The Albert Kennedy Trust
Nationwide
www.akt.org.uk/wedding

TheGiftListCompany.com
www.thegiftlistcompany.com

Charity Gift List – Give It
Hertfordshire
www.giveit.co.uk

Honeymoon Gift Lists – SendUsPacking
Ltd
Cotswolds/ Gloucestershire
www.SendUsPacking.com

John Lewis
www.johnlewis.com

LEGAL MATTERS

Sue Elkington, Pink Wills
Birmingham
www.pink-wills.com

Russell Jones & Walker Solicitors
www.rjw.co.uk

Rainbowsure.com
Insurance company, Manchester
www.rainbowsure.com

PHOTOGRAPHERS & VIDEOGRAPHERS

Andy Webb Photography
Surrey
www.andywebbphotography.com

AMD Photography
Surrey
www.amdphotography.co.uk

Julia Boggio Photography
London
www.juliaboggiophotography.com

Blenheim Photography Ltd
Highnam
www.blenheimphotography.co.uk

Bostick Photography
East Sussex
www.bostickphotography.com

Faye Collyer, trading as Phase
Photographic
Hove
www.phasephotographic.com

Nigel Copcutt Photography
Petersfield
www.nigelcopcutt.co.uk

Cut Mustard TV
Videographers, Scotland
www.cutmustard.tv

FX Films
Videographers, Hampshire
www.fxfilms.co.uk

Damian Hall Photography
West Yorkshire
www.damianhall.com

Thomas Haywood
Photographer, Edinburgh
www.thomashaywood.com

Hoult Images Photography
Oxfordshire
www.hiwp.co.uk

IKONOGRAPHY
Liverpool
www.ikonography.net

In the Pink
Cheshire
www.inthepinkphotography.com

Leahphotography
Cardiff
www.leahphotography.co.uk

Esther Ling Photography
Norfolk
www.estherling.co.uk

David McNeil photography
London
www.davidmmcneil.com

Nuptialis
Essex
www.nuptialisfilms.co.uk

Matt Pereira Photography
Hampshire
www.mattpereira.co.uk

Pride Photography
Bristol
www.pridephotographyonline.co.uk

John Stevens
Photographer, Brighton
www.johnestevens.com

Takeone Photography
Northeast
www.takeonephotography.org.uk

Angela Wynne Photographer
Manchester
www.angelawynne.com

PUBLICATIONS

Attitude Magazine
nationwide
www.attitude.co.uk

DIVA Magazine
www.diva-mag.co.uk

Gay Times magazine
www.gaytimes.co.uk

Pink Paper
www.pinkpaper.com

Pride Life
www.pridelife.co.uk

Outnorthwest magazine (The Lesbian and Gay Foundation)
Manchester
www.lgf.org.uk

Out in the City Magazine
www.outmag.co.uk

The Gay Wedding Organizer
Worcestershire
www.gayweddingorganizer.co.uk

STATIONERY & FAVOURS

Acushla Creations
Manchester
www.acushlacreations.co.uk

Ciano
West Midlands
www.ciano.org.uk

Country Party
Nationwide
www.countryparty.co.uk

Lets-Celebrate
Cheshire
www.lets-celebrate.co.uk

Pink Wedding Stationery
Online
www.pinkweddingstationery.co.uk

So Inviting
Hand-crafted stationery, Cardiff
www.soinviting.co.uk

Sticky Snail Design
Cheshire
www.stickysnaildesign.co.uk

Thorntons Direct
Nationwide
www.thorntons.co.uk

TOASTMASTERS

Ian Low Toastmaster
Kent
www.ianlowtoastmaster.co.uk

National Association of Toastmasters
www.natuk.com

Tilmanstone Toastmasters
Kent
www.tilmanstonetoastmasters.co.uk

TRANSPORT

A & L Griffiths Chauffeur and wedding cars
Cardiff
www.algriffiths.co.uk

Blush Hospitality
London and Home counties
www.blush-hospitality.com

Mark Scotts Wedding Car Hire
Surrey
www.surrey-wedding-car-hire.co.uk

WeddingBelle Ltd
Pontypool
www.weddingbelle.biz

TRAVEL/HONEYMOONS

Foreign and Commonwealth Office
www.fco.gov.uk/en/travelling-and-living-overseas

PLANitGAY
www.planitgay.com

Purple Roofs
www.purpleroofs.com

WEDDING RINGS

Bliss Rings
Kent
www.blissrings.co.uk

Clive Ranger
Cardiff
www.cliveranger.co.uk

Love and Pride
www.loveandpride.com

Symply Bands
www.symjewellery.co.uk

Touch Wood Rings
British Columbia, Canada
www.touchwoodrings.com

TOP 10 UK DESTINATIONS FOR CIVIL PARTNERSHIP CEREMONIES

Here is the Top 10 list of areas that registered Civil Partnerships in 2007.

TOP 10 AREAS IN ENGLAND IN 2007

1. Westminster, London
2. Brighton and Hove
3. Kensington and Chelsea, London
4. Kent
5. Islington, London
6. Manchester
7. Norfolk
8. Surrey
9. Hampshire
10. Birmingham

MOST DESIRABLE AREAS IN THE UK

Here is the list of areas registering the most number of Civil Partnerships since it became law.

TOP 10 AREAS IN THE UK FROM DECEMBER 2005 TO 2007

1. Brighton and Hove
2. Westminster, London
3. Kensington and Chelsea, London
4. Kent
5. Islington, London
6. Edinburgh
7. Manchester
8. Hampshire
9. Surrey
10. Norfolk

England
Based on these figures, Brighton and Hove have led the way overall, arguably proving to be the 'all-time' top destination for Civil Partnerships across the UK. Brighton has a proud reputation of being the UK's gay capital by the sea.

Wales
Cardiff retained its first position in 2007 by holding about 50 percent more Civil Partnerships than Swansea, which came in second. Cardiff is known for its famous cosmopolitan feel. In Wales, you will also come across some of the most fascinating castles and heritage sites the UK has to offer.

Scotland
In 2007, the capital city, Edinburgh, registered around 40 percent more Civil Partnerships ceremonies than second place Glasgow, with 535 and 386 respectively. Edinburgh has one of the loveliest cityscapes in the world, and has a great mix of new and old venues, leaving you spoilt for choice.

Northern Ireland
In 2007, Eastern Northern Ireland remained ahead of the Western area for registered Civil Partnerships by 80 percent. Northern Ireland has always been famous for its history, legends and the genuine warmth of the local people. This list shows our Pink Approved venues around the UK that are working in partnership with Pink Weddings™ Ltd.

PINK WEDDINGS™ TOP 10 HONEYMOON DESTINATIONS

1. Canada
2. Gran Canaria
3. United States of America
4. South Africa
5. Italy
6. Australia
7. Netherlands
8. Thailand
9. Spain
10. Mexico

PINK WEDDINGS™ VENUE RECOMMENDATIONS

See Pink Weddings™ website for full listings.

BERKSHIRE
The Crowne Plaza, Reading
www.crowneplaza.co.uk
The Harte & Garter Hotel & Spa,
Windsor
ww.foliohotels.com/harteandgarter
Reading Moathouse
www.bw-readingmoathouse.co.uk
The Renaissance Reading Hotel
www.pentahotels.com/en/reading-gb
BUCKINGHAMSHIRE
The Bull Hotel, Gerrards Cross
www.sarova.com/bull
DEVON
Elfordleigh Hotel, Golf and Leisure
www.elfordleigh.co.uk
DORSET
Village Hotel, Bournemouth
www.village-hotels.co.uk
ESSEX
Fennes Estate, Braintree
www.fennes.co.uk
Hylands House, Chelmsford
Tel: + 44 (0) 1245605500
Parklands Quendon Hall
www.quendonpark.co.uk
GLOUCESTERSHIRE
Great Tythe Barn, Tetbury
www.gtb.co.uk
Matara, Kingscote
www.matara.co.uk
Ramada Bowden Hall
www.ramadajarvis.co.uk
HAMPSHIRE
Audleys Wood, Basingstoke
www.handpicked.co.uk
Hilton Hotel, Basingstoke
www.hilton.co.uk/basingstoke
The Holiday Inn, Southampton
www.holidayinn.com
Marwell Hotel, Winchester
www.marwellhotel.co.uk
Marwell Zoological Park
www.marwell.org.uk
Oakley Hall, Basingstoke
www.oakleyhall-park.com
Potters Heron Hotel, Romsey
Tel: + 44 (0) 2380277800
Rhinefield House Hotel, Brockenhurst
www.handpicked.co.uk
Ramada Farnham
www.ramadajarvis.co.uk

HERTFORDSHIRE
Buckettslands Farm, Well End
www.buckettslandfarm.com
IRELAND
Tinakilly Country House –
South of Dublin
www.tinakilly.ie
KENT
Brandshatch Hotel & Spa, Fawkham
www.handpicked.co.uk
Chilston Park Hotel, Maidstone
www.handpicked.co.uk
Cooling Castle Barn, Rochester
www.coolingcastlebarn.com
The Lordswood Centre, Chatham
www.lordswood-leisure.co.uk
Marriott Tudor Park, Maidstone
www.marriott.co.uk/hotels
Philpots Manor, Hildenborough
Tel: + 44 (0) 1732833047
The Ramada Hotel and Resort,
Maidstone
www.ramadajarvis.co.uk
The Royal Oak, Brookland
www.royaloakbrookland.co.uk
Village Hotel and Leisure Club,
Maidstone
www.village-hotels.co.uk
LANCASHIRE
The Ramada, Bolton
www.ramadajarvis.co.uk
Hotel Elizabeth North Euston
www.elizabethhotels.co.uk
LINCOLNSHIRE
De Vere, Belton Woods
www.devere-hotels.com
LONDON
Andaz Hotel
www.Andaz.com
Bingham, Richmond Upon Thames
www.thebingham.co.uk
Cannizaro House, Wimbledon
www.cannizarohouse.com
City Inn, Westminster
www.cityinn.com/london
Holiday Inn, Kensington
Holiday Inn, Brentford Lock
Holiday Inn, Camden Lock
www.holidayinn.com
One Great George Street
www.onegreatgeorgestreet.com
The Ramada, Hyde Park

The Ramada, Ealing
www.ramadajarvis.co.uk
The Rookery, Clerkenwell
www.hazlittshotel.com
GREATER MANCHESTER
The Ramada Jarvis, Piccadilly Hotel
www.ramadajarvis.co.uk
Haigh Hall, Wigan
www.haighhall.net
MIDDLESEX
The Ship Hotel, Shepperton
www.theshiphotel
shepperton.co.uk
The Holiday Inn London-
Shepperton
www.holidayinn.com
NATIONWIDE
The National Trust
www.nationaltrust.org.uk
NEWCASTLE
Village Hotel and Leisure Club
www.villagehotels.co.uk
NORFOLK
The Cliff Hotel, Great Yarmouth
www.elizabethhotels.co.uk
NORTHAMPTONSHIRE
Highgate House, Northampton
www.sundialgroup.com
OXFORDSHIRESHIRE
Luxters, Henley-on-Thames
www.oldluxtersbarn.co.uk
RUTLAND
The Whipper In, Oakham
Tel: + 44 (0) 1572756971
SCOTLAND
Swallow Hotel, Dundee
www.swallow-hotels.com
The Gables Hotel, Gretna Green
www.gables-hotel-gretna.co.uk
The Hub, Edinburgh
www.thehub-edinburgh.com
Guthrie Castle, Angus
www.guthriecastle.com
Glenmoriston Town House,
Inverness
www.glenmoristontown
house.com
The Lodge, Edinburgh
www.thelodgehotel.co.uk
The National Trust for Scotland
www.nts.org.uk
SOMERSET
Holbrook House, Wincanton
www.holbrookhouse.co.uk
SURREY
Addington Palace

www.addington-palace.co.uk
Barnett Hill, Guildford
www.sundialgroup.com
Oatlands Park Hotel, Weybridge
www.oatlandsparkhotel.com
SUFFOLK
Hotel Elizabeth Orwell, Felixstowe
www.elizabethhotels.co.uk
Best Western Hotel, Hatfield
www.bestwestern.co.uk
SUSSEX
Alias Seattle Hotel, Brighton
www.aliashotels.com/seattle
The Angel Hotel, Midhurst
www.theangelmidhurst.co.uk
Deans Place, Alfriston
www.deansplacehotel.co.uk
Hilton Brighton Metropole
www.hilton.co.uk/brighton.met
The Ramada, Brighton
www.ramadajarvis.co.uk
WALES
Craig y Nos Castle, Powys
www.craigynoscastle.com
Village Hotel, Swansea
www.village-hotels.co.uk
WEST MIDLANDS
The Macdonald Burlington Hotel
www.macdonaldhotels.co.uk
Marston Farm Hotel, Sutton
Coldfield
www.marstonfarm-hotel.co.uk
New Hall, Birmingham
www.handpicked.co.uk
The Ramada Hotel and Resort,
Birmingham
The Ramada Hotel, Solihull
The Ramada, Newton Park
www.ramadajarvis.co.uk
Woodside House, Kenilworth
www.sundialgroup.com
WILTSHIRE
The Guildhall, Salisbury
www.salisburyguildhall.co.uk
YORKSHIRE
The George Hotel, Huddersfield
www.thegeorgehotel
huddersfield.co.uk
Hotel Elizabeth, Hull
www.elizabethhotels.co.uk
Merrion Hotel, Leeds
www.brook-hotels.co.uk/
merrion_hotel.html
The Ramada, Leeds
The Ramada, Wetherby
www.ramadajarvis.co.uk

INDEX